Second Edition

ACCOUNTING FOR GROWTH

*Stripping the camouflage
from Company Accounts*

Terry Smith

**RANDOM HOUSE
BUSINESS BOOKS**

This edition first published by Century Ltd
Random House, 20 Vauxhall Bridge Road, London SW1V 2SA

Random House Australia (Pty) Limited
16 Dalmore Drive, Scoresby
Victoria 3179, Australia

Random House New Zealand Limited
18 Poland Road, Glenfield
Auckland 10, New Zealand

Random House South Africa (Pty) Limited
Box 2263, Rosebank 2121, South Africa
Random House UK Limited Reg. No. 954009

Papers used by Random House UK Limited are natural, recyclable products made
from wood grown in sustainable forests. The manufacturing processes conform to
the environmental regulations of the country of origin.

ISBN 0 7126 7594 9

Typeset by SX Composing DTP, Rayleigh, Essex
Printed and bound in Great Britain by Mackays of Chatham plc, Chatham, Kent

Companies, institutions and other organizations wishing to make bulk purchases
of any business books published by Random House should contact their local
bookseller or Random House direct:
Special Sales Director
Random House, 20 Vauxhall Bridge Road, London SW1V 2SA
tel 0171 973 9000 Fax 0171 828 6681

Contents

Acknowledgements

My list of acknowledgements for this second edition of Accounting for Growth is shorter than in the first edition in some respects and longer in others.

It is shorter because I had comparatively little help on this occasion in preparing the book. All of the new material for the book has been accumulated by me over the period since the first edition.

But my acknowledgements must be longer in that without the help of some individuals there would be no second edition, and indeed the first edition might never have seen the light of day. I refer of course to those who supported me after I was fired and sued because of the publication of *Accounting for Growth* in August 1992. They include my wife Barbara. Despite all the traumas which were caused by the publication of the book she never once faltered in her support or suggested that I should bow to pressure. Also David Poutney, my longest standing and closest friend and colleague. David left UBS after I was fired to become my partner again at Collins Stewart & Co. My solicitor Seamus Smyth who never wavered in defending me. My new partners and colleagues at Collins Stewart & Co who took me into their business after I was fired, and have encouraged me to write this second edition. I must also mention those clients who have given me business at my new firm and made me feel that the fight was worthwhile. And last but by no means least, those in the press who gave me a fair hearing.

Without their contribution, this book would not exist.

TCS
May 1996

Part I

Introduction and Background to the Second Edition

1

A FUNNY THING HAPPENED ON THE WAY TO THE PUBLISHERS

Hollow vessels make the greatest sound
Anon

That plus 10 cents and you get a ride on the subway
New Yorkers' saying

It may help to bring readers up to date about this book if I begin with some of the extraordinary events in the summer of 1992. After the original research report in early 1991, preparation of the book and publication went ahead uneventfully and do not deserve comment. It was not publication that caused the excitement in 1992, but the attempts to suppress the book completely.

I have already explained in the first edition how I was prompted to write the book by the even more extraordinary events in the UK economy and stock market in 1990-92. In my opinion, these events were due to more than just the impact of a ferocious recession given additional impetus by the reaction to events in Kuwait in the summer of 1990. UK quoted companies had begun to drop like ninepins, and I was struck by the extent to which investors, even professional fund managers and analysts, were quite naive in thinking that published company accounts were in some way a protection against losing money in this maelstrom. I am producing a second and updated edition because I am not much less impressed by their naïveté today, as you will see from the BTR example which I quote in Chapter 4 and on page 189.

I wrote the book in a particular format: with lots of examples taken from company accounts. There had been works on creative accounting before, such as Ian Griffiths' *Creative Accounting* but they had generally failed to name names, relying instead upon using examples of 'Company A' and 'Company B'. I felt that readers should be able to use the book to look at live (and dead) company examples in order to give them a realistic guide as to what to look for. This presented an obvious problem. The original report had caused some stirrings in the undergrowth from companies which were unhappy about being included. Now some were alerted to the fact that there was a book on the way.

After the manuscript had been completed, submitted to the publishers and proof-read, the attempt to suppress the book took off. The first contact was from Tiphook, the container leasing company which had featured in the original research report and was now in the book. Representations were made by Tiphook's Chairman, Robert Montagu (subsequently declared bankrupt) to suggest that Tiphook should be dropped as an example.

Figure 1.1 Tiphook (Central Transport Rental) share price relative to the All Share Index 1992-96

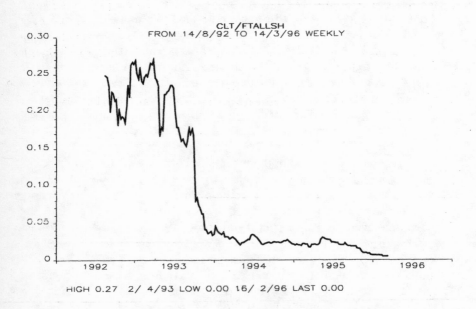

But Montagu did not have enough clout to cause a real problem. That came when Grand Met discovered from preliminary press reviews that it was the company with the most 'blobs' in the notorious 'Major Companies Accounting Health Check' table, or as it become known, the Blob Guide. Out of twelve techniques examined in the first edition, Grand Met was listed as using nine, the largest number for any company in the Top 200. It is a supreme irony that after the first edition was published and I was fired and sued I had to check the accuracy of a number of entries including Grand Met's and found that I had missed one: Grand Met was using ten techniques!

Grand Met took a dim view of this and pressure was brought to bear by Allen Sheppard and, when this did not succeed, by Colin Marshall, a non executive director of Grand Met, but more crucially, then Chief Executive of British Airways. I was then told to stop publication of the book completely. Apart from my wishes in the matter, everyone seemed to have overlooked a small difficulty in achieving this: it was no longer my book and I had no control over it. I had already sold the book to my publisher. He now both possessed and owned the book, and owed me the royalties. Contacting a publisher and asking him to stop publication was not only a highly unusual step for an author to take, it was also likely to make him (or her) have the commercial equivalent of an orgasm. Publicity sells books (some people seemed to have overlooked the common roots between the words 'publisher' and 'publicity') as anyone who had followed the case of the British Government's attempts to block the publication of *Spycatcher* would have known. Telling a publisher not to publish because there was a row brewing was a bit like giving someone a tanker full of petrol with which to extinguish a fire. Whoosh!

Figure 1.2   Grand Met share price relative to the All Share Index 1992-96

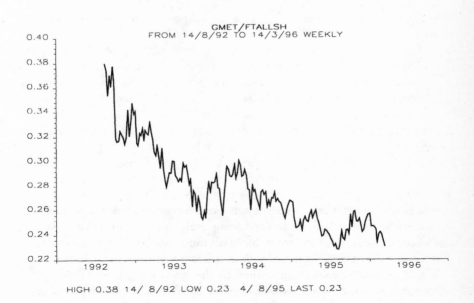

The rest, as they say, is history. The book was published. I was fired and sued. The book received more publicity than Random House could probably have purchased with its entire advertising budget. Analysts woke up to the issue of creative accounting in general, and in companies such as Grand Met and Tiphook in particular:

A very curious episode in my life then unfolded. Apart from deciding what to do for the rest of my working life, and fighting a substantial law suit, I was also engaged on a speaking tour which took me around the UK and to Ireland and France, speaking about creative accounting. This was enjoyable, but some curious episodes occurred. I refer in particular to one conference at which I was confronted by a speaker from accountants Ernst & Young. Ernst & Young were the only firm which had gone on record at the time of publication to condemn the book as 'dangerous and irresponsible'. The press seemed to have overlooked the coincidence that Ernst & Young were a) UBS's auditors; and b) the only firm of accountants named in the book. It is amazing how these coincidences go unremarked: UBS became brokers to Tiphook after I was fired, despite the fact that their Transport analyst (one Richard Hannah would you believe, the co-author of the original 'Accounting for Growth' research report) had been a constant critic of the company. Anyway, the Ernst & Young speaker proceeded to berate me for producing a book that was inaccurate and too simplistic. In its place he recommended Ernst & Young's publication *UK GAAP* ('Generally Accepted Accounting Practice') the current edition of which ran to some 1,226 pages of technical analysis.

When I was able to set aside my feeling of surprise that any UK accountant should have the gall to criticise someone else's work as misleading in the light of various episodes concerning the accountancy profession in recent years which are almost too numerous to mention, I was able to agree that *UK GAAP* and a host of other books are much better technical guides to UK accounting than *Accounting for Growth*. My reason for labouring this incident is that I want the opportunity to reiterate the reasons behind the publication of this book and its target audience in this second edition. At its simplest, if I wanted to write a book on accounting which was useful to senior technical partners of Ernst & Young, my royalty account would be a lot smaller. Moreover, I wanted to write a book that would help laymen to understand what was going on. The average person who is sufficiently interested in investment to read a book on accounting is not likely to select a 1,226 page manual.

But there was an even more important difference bewteen *UK GAAP* and *Accounting for Growth* which the man from Ernst & Young seemed to miss, in common with a lot of professionals. A frequent defence which is heard when any company's accounting is criticised is "but it [the treatment being adopted] is allowed within UK GAAP."

To my knowledge none of the companies named in the first edition nor any of the companies in this second edition are in breach of UK GAAP in the treatments they are using and which I highlight. But as they say in New York "that plus 10 cents and you get a ride on the subway". Or to put it in English: so what? It is quite possible to lose money if a company's accounts follow UK GAAP to the letter, but the picture presented is so misleading that you are unable to interpret them correctly and as a result fail to see that it is financially vulnerable or its earnings are unsustainable.

As anyone who has read the first edition will know, in this book I try to give a quote at the beginning of each chapter which gives some clue to its contents. Well at least now you know the context to the second quote for this chapter, but what about empty vessels making the greatest sound? The share price charts for Tiphook and Grand Met obviously give me some pride, and not just because their executives caused me some needless problems. I also got some clients to sell the shares and so avoid losses. A book is not a finely timed instrument like a piece of broker's research which can be produced literally overnight, and may have a very short shelf life. The predictions and rules in a book may take longer to work, but they should also pass the test of time.

I must leave you, the reader, to decide whether this is true of *Accounting for Growth*, but with all due respect to the gentlemen (and ladies) from Ernst & Young I reproduce below an article from *The Sunday Times* in November 1993, which looks at the fate of some of the high scorers in the blob guide as a contribution to the debate. The 'blob guide' was never intended to be a precise instrument of analysis, since for example it makes no attempt to weight the size or impact of the accounting techniques utilised, and if anything I am surprised at how successful it has been given these obvious limitations. It was only ever intended as a warning to the reader to examine the accounts of any company listed.

So how does this explain empty vessels? If I were running a public company, and some analyst decided to criticise my company's accounts, I like to believe that if I knew he was wrong I would not rail against him in public or call his boss and demand a retraction or his dismissal. Rather I would smile knowingly and hope the poor misguided fellow drove the company's share price down so that I could buy a few more. In my experience, when companies start issuing threats, and bringing back door pressure to bear to stop criticism, this is a better indicator that something is wrong than all of the blob guides, UK GAAP books, analysts' circulars and charts put together.

Pleasant reading.

The maverick analyst who went to war with the City and won

Terry Smith was vilified for his book on company accounts. But the downfall of Queens Moat, Trafalgar and Tiphook has proved him right.

FIFTEEN MONTHS after Terry Smith's controversial book, Accounting for Growth, climbed into the bestseller lists, event after event is proving the maverick analyst right.

Three of the most notable corporate disasters of the year – Queens Moat Houses, the hotels group; Tiphook, the container and trailer rental company; and Trafalgar House, the contracting and construction firm now controlled by Hongkong Land – were highlighted in the book for their dubious accounting practices. Smith, now working at Collins Stewart, the boutique broker, can barely suppress a smile.

"Tiphook, if you look back on it, was frighteningly obvious," he says. "The amazing thing is that UBS then took the company on as a client."

UBS, the Swiss bank where Smith was the head of research until he was removed from the premises after refusing to scrap his book, is pressing ahead with its case for alleged breach of copyright. Smith has responded with a claim for unfair dismissal. The bank denies it objected to the book because of pressure from clients, and claims Smith broke house rules by failing to check facts with the companies concerned before publishing.

A trial is due to begin next October, and "discovery" of documents continued in the High Court last week.

Smith has spent an estimated £170,000 on legal bills and, with Singer & Friedlander, the merchant bank, offering financial backing, is ready and willing to press on. His financial resources are meagre against those of UBS, one of the world's banking giants, but UBS has discovered its opponent is nothing if not determined. Sources say attempts by the Swiss bank to settle out of court have been turned down.

Smith is keeping a close eye on the companies that he says tried to intervene to have the book abandoned or their names deleted from it.

"It is fascinating to watch the performance of those companies that tried to get the book stopped," he says. Sir Allen Sheppard's Grand Metropolitan, which topped Smith's list for the highest number of dubious accounting methods, was among those to complain to UBS. "Since then GrandMet shares have significantly under-performed the rest of the market," he points out.

Inntrepreneur, GrandMet's pub joint venture with Courage, now finds its loans listed by at least one merchant bank as "distressed debt", selling for only a portion of their full face value, a status usually reserved for companies acknowledged to be facing financial difficulties. Debt in the loss-making Inntrepreneur does not sell at the heavy discounts to book value reached by Gerald Ronson's Heron Group, for example, but Smith believes Inntrepreneur's debt is uncomfortably high.

Robert Montague, chairman of Tiphook, was another to express his unhappiness. Tiphook is now holding talks with its bankers after gearing soared to more than 500%.

How Smith's culprits came unstuck
Companies using the most dubious accounting practices

Tiphook (4)	In talks with banks, debts soar
Queens Moat (6)	Financial reconstruction under way
Trafalgar House (8)	Auditors, chairman and chief executive depart; huge losses, two rights issues
Albert Fisher (7)	Losses, chairman departs
British Aerospace (7)	Record losses, rights issue
Ratners (7)	Founder departs, huge losses
Lonrho (6)	Huge changes in way group is run
GrandMet (9)	Shares underperform
Bass (6)	Shares underperform
Ladbroke (8)	Chairman steps down

Trafalgar House became one of the highest-profile cases of dubious accounting when it was forced to re-issue accounts after a protracted inquiry by the Financial Review Panel.

When first published, Smith's book was criticised as superficial and an unreliable guide to company accounts. Ernst & Young, an accountant with several clients among Smith's list of worst offenders, dismissed the book as "dangerous and irresponsible". Others (including The Sunday Times, which published extracts), welcomed Smith's method of bringing the usually dry issue of accountancy methods into the open.

"Terry identified exactly the same problems as we did with the accountancy world," says Professor David Tweedie, head of the Accounting Standards Board. "I think of the 12 issues he highlighted we have now dealt with nine of them." Certainly investors who avoided companies covered in the book would be much better off today.

In his new job, Smith now specialises in targeting and analysing companies that may be facing financial difficulties.

Just over a year ago, Smith questioned the apparent infallibility of Spring Ram, then a highly successful kitchens and bathrooms group. This year, the edifice began to crumble and the company is now facing severe financial difficulties. "There were some very obvious superficial signals that the company had lost touch with its business," he says. "The annual report was full of sportsmen wearing Spring Ram shirts, but there were no pictures of bathrooms."

A trigger for further investigations is high profit margins. "If they are achieving improbable margins they are probably doing something wrong. There has to be a logical explanation." Polly Peck was an obvious example.

A company to watch, he suggests, is BTR, because it is muddying its accounting methods rather than cleaning them up. "We all understood where BTR used to get its 15% margins from because they were outstanding industrial managers," he says. "But the acquisition accounting on their purchase of Hawker Siddeley was as bad as I have ever seen. It is now like trying to view something through a smokescreen."

Article by Kirstie Hamilton, *The Sunday Times*, 14 November 1993.

2

WHAT HAS HAPPENED SINCE 1992?

A girl writes home from her boarding school to her parents. Her letter tells them that there has been a fire in her dormitory. Her parents are obviously worried by this news. But the letter goes on to say that she was rescued by the school handyman. She has forged a strong friendship with the handyman as a result. So strong in fact that she is pregnant by him and they have eloped. Her parents are aghast until they read the postcript which says: "None of the foregoing actually happened. I just failed my History GCSE and wanted you to get it in perspective."

Joke told by Sir David Tweedie, Chairman of the ASB. The punchline is always to 'Look for the bottom line' including in letters.

It brings home the need for this second edition for me to realise that the Accounting Standards Board (ASB) had only just issued its first Financial Reporting Standard (FRS) – FRS 1 when the first edition was published. In fact a question which I have often been asked at seminars and conferences is something along the lines of: is there really any need for your book now that we have the ASB? To some extent, this new edition attempts to answer that question by looking at the state of company accounting after all the ASB has achieved.

The foundation of the ASB under Sir David Tweedie was a recognition that there was a great deal wrong with UK accounting. Tweedie has set about correcting this with an almost evangelical zeal. And he tells good jokes. It does not do full justice to his achievements at the ASB simply to list its published standards. But nonetheless here goes:

Financial Reporting Standards (FRS)

FRS 1	Cash Flow Statements
FRS 2	Accounting for Subsidiary Undertakings
FRS 3	Reporting Financial Performance
FRS 4	Capital Instruments
FRS 5	Reporting the Substance of Transactions
FRS 6	Acquisitions and Mergers
FRS 7	Fair Values in Acquisition Accountancy
FRS 8	Related party disclosures

For the non technical reader, the contents of some of these Standards is almost impossible to predict from the title. Take FRS 3. 'Reporting Financial Performance' could cover almost anything.

Many of this series of new FRS' relate precisely to areas mentioned in the first edition, and will be covered in some detail in the following chapters. There are also a number of discussion papers and exposure drafts which will become new Standards, such as those dealing with pension funds, goodwill and deferred taxation; these are covered in the later chapters in which we look forward to new developments in accounting and the effects which they may have on companies.

In addition the Urgent Issues Task Force (UITF) has also issued Abstracts ostensibly clarifying existing standards, but in reality often changing the way companies are able to draw up their accounts in response to some of the grosser abuses which have been perpetrated. Two that we shall look at which have had a profound effect are UITF Abstract 3: Treatment of goodwill on disposal of a business, and Abstract 5: Transfers from current assets to fixed assets.

It is not, however, the aim of this second edition to stand in judgement on the ASB's work, but rather just to update readers on some loopholes which have been closed since 1992, and some new ones which have opened. There is little doubt that the ASB has achieved a great deal in making UK accounting more rigorous, but there is equally little doubt that their task will never be finished in any normal sense. David Tweedie himself in his more candid moments confesses that his job is a bit like painting the Forth Bridge. Once it is finished you start all over again. He realised that whatever rules you put in place, smart people will find a way to express a distorted or flattering picture of their performance. He recognises that the ASB will in that sense always be one step behind. The Forth Bridge aspect of his work is brought home by the fact that as I prepare this second edition, the ASB has just issued FRED ('Financial Reporting Exposure Draft') 10 with its revisions to FRS 1. This is designed to solve some of the problems which quickly became apparent in the implementation of this first Standard. That if you like is the bottom line to what the ASB has achieved to date: better accounting standards, but they cannot remain ossified for all time, and neither could *Accounting for Growth*.

Some of the chapters from the first edition have been unaffected by the ASB's reforms, and so have survived almost in their entirety. These are:

Deferred Consideration (Chapter 6); Contingent Liabilities (Chapter 9); Capitalisation of Costs (Chapter 10); Brand Accounting (Chapter 11); Changes in Depreciation Policy (Chapter 12); Currency Mismatching (Chapter 14) and Pension Fund Accounting (Chapter 15).

However, in some cases they have been modified to take account of developments since 1992. Examples are the chapter on Depreciation, which now includes some material on the debate about the depreciation of properties, and on Pension Fund Accounting which includes the proposals in the ASB's Discussion Paper. In other cases new examples have been introduced, such as the example of Quality Software Products in the chapter on Capitalisation of Costs and a review of information on Hanson's interest rate arbitrage activities in the chapter on Currency Mismatching.

Other chapters have ceased to have any significance as a result of the new Financial Reporting Standards. For example, FRS 3 basically outlawed extraordinary items and thereby rendered Chapter 7 in the first edition redundant. But it has been replaced by a new chapter on the operation of FRS 3. The reader will find that in common with other chapters, it does not give a detailed description of FRS 3. It is instead meant to serve as a short and hopefully readable guide to those aspects of the operation of FRS 3 which may affect the investor.

Similarly, all of the techniques described in the old chapters on Off Balance Sheet Finance and Convertibles With Put Options and AMPs have effectively been dealt with by FRS 2, FRS 4 and FRS 5. There are still companies with weird and wonderful capital instruments and assets and, more important, liabilities in off balance sheet structures. But reporting of these items has been tightened so that there is now less chance for companies to shift items off their reported group balance sheet, the main purpose of which is to understate the gearing. Beyond a certain point, the higher a company's gearing, the lower its equity should be rated because the existence of high gearing can be a threat to the equity holders' capital and income. For example, FRS 2 brought the definition of a subsidiary in accounting standards into line with the Companies Acts. It widened the definition of control to bring the sort of 'non subsidiary subsidiary' route used by the likes of LEP with St Pauls Vista (see chapter 8 in the first edition) with their property assets and borrowings back on to the group balance sheet, often with disastrous effects.

Some chapters have required heavy modification as a result of the ASB's reforms, such as the chapters on Acquisition Accounting and Disposals. The opportunity has also been taken to introduce new examples into these chapters from the period since 1992 in order to bring them up to date.

Chapters have also been introduced on entirely new areas of accounting which have become topical as a result of developments since 1992, such as Cash Flow Accounting, and Transfers from Current Assets to Fixed Assets.

In general, an effort has been made to shorten the chapters since 1992. This is partly because accounting remains a subject which few people will read about for pleasure, so my view is that the less you have to read to get the essence of a subject, the better. But in contrast it is worth noting that there are chapters dealing with fifteen techniques of so-called creative accounting in this edition versus a dozen in 1992. Perhaps this is a reflection of the remaining opportunities to 'cook the books' even after all the ASB's reforms? It certainly emphasises the need for constant vigilance if you are not to be parted from your money.

After the chapters on creative techniques, the Major Companies Accounting Health Check has been dropped. Although it was a popular item in the 1992 edition and caused great controversy, it always suffered from the shortcomings of an admittedly simplistic approach. Instead, the chapter on Survival Techniques has been heavily modified with some of the previous hints, such as watching for transfers between the balance sheet and profit & loss account and cash flow, given chapters of their own in order to do justice to developments since 1992. As a replacement for the old 'blob guide' the Survival Techniques chapter also touches upon a system for predicting company failure, a subject to which I intend to return in more detail in my next book.

3

THE 1980s – THE DECADE OF THE DEAL – AND THE 1990s

Q. How do you become big in the corporate finance business?
A. Start 20 years ago.

Liberalisation and *laissez faire*
Economic growth and Thatcherite deregulation combined with a raging bull market in equities and an easy supply of credit were a recipe for a booming market in houses and take-overs, and that is what the 1980s saw, particularly in the United States and the UK. In the UK, the take-over fires were fanned by a number of factors. Together these created a situation in which the 1980s have come to be known as 'the decade of the deal'. Icons of the age, many of which have since fallen, included the eponymous Donald Trump, who even wrote a book called *The Art of the Deal*.

First among these factors was a Government committed to the freedom of the markets and to financial liberalisation. This saw an end to Exchange Controls, which helped to fuel cross-border investment and take-over activity, and the imposition (for that is effectively what it was) of Big Bang on the cosy cartel which constituted the London Stock Exchange. This in turn led to the disappearance of most traditional stockbroking firms into integrated securities houses complete with expensive corporate finance departments keen to justify their existence. This is an important factor to realise because there is no doubt that many of the deals which grabbed the headlines, particularly towards the end of the 1980s, were hatched in the City's corporate finance departments.

It is no surprise that some of the most spectacular disasters involved the new generation of integrated houses rather than the established mergers and acquisitions players, such as the merchant banks Schroders or Warburgs, and Rowe & Pitman or Cazenove amongst the brokers. There is a saying in the investment world that if you want to be big in the corporate finance business you need to start twenty years ago. What it means is that there is no substitute for connections, judgement and even integrity. But that did not stop the new integrated houses trying. They backed the upstarts of the corporate world with their leveraged bids and grandiose schemes, for the more traditional, i.e. safe, corporate clients were mostly closed to them. So it was that Barclays de Zoete Wedd were advisers to the ill-fated British & Commonwealth, and County NatWest to Tony Berry's Blue Arrow. Probably the single most important word in the corporate finance business is 'No' – when said to a client to explain why his deal will not work and cannot be backed. But it is a word which can cost a firm clients since it is one which thrusting entrepreneurs and captains of industry are not accustomed to hearing. Only those with an existing sound corporate list of clients can risk telling a John Gunn that British & Commonwealth should not take over Atlantic Computers, or Tony Berry that they cannot get the institutions to take the shares he needs to issue to buy Manpower. The new integrated houses appeared not to have faith in their corporate client lists. Had someone said the word 'No' they might have saved Messrs Gunn, Berry and their investors a literal fortune.

Hand in hand with the Government's liberalisation of the financial markets was the *laissez faire* attitude to the resulting upsurge in take-over activity, particularly from the mid-1980s. Virtually no one was safe from the rigours of the market. Household names such as Rowntree were gobbled up by the Swiss. Jaguar was driven into American hands and what was left of the British computer hardware industry (ICL and Apricot) was consumed by the Japanese. This trend has revived in the mid 1990s, with Rover being sold to BMW, and most of the UK securities industry and the newly privatised regional electricity companies (RECs) disappearing into often foreign hands.

Through all this upheaval, the Bank of England was relaxed, but stood firm on one issue, which was to protect the clearing banks from anyone who was not "fit and proper" – polite language for anyone who was 1) foreign, or 2) might inject some commercial reality into those most unloved of British institutions. But even the Bank of England could not resist the take-over tide completely and there were plenty of sacrificial lambs amongst the merchant banks as Hill Samuel was swallowed by TSB, Guinness Mahon by the New Zealand-based Equiticorp, and Morgan Grenfell by Deutsche Bank. The fact that Equiticorp quickly went bust and was engaged in a share support operation suggests that the definition of fit and proper could be stretched to include foreigners with improbable finances if they were willing to relieve the Bank of England of a potential problem.

As a result, Hongkong Bank, which had been barred from taking over The Royal Bank of Scotland by the Bank of England in 1981 allegedly because the Bank was concerned about standards of banking supervision in Hong Kong (some rich irony here given the Bank's own experience of matters such as Johnson Matthey Bankers, BCCI and more recently, Barings), was eventually able to gain control of Midland Bank when the recovery plans of Sir Kit McMahon (himself a former Deputy Governor of the Bank of England) were torpedoed by the recession.

Indeed, although the 1990s are shaping up in a remarkably similar fashion to the 1980s given the take-over boom in 1995, they are different in at least one respect: the waning influence of the Bank of England in protecting its flock from take-over. Apart from Midland, TSB did not last a decade as a quoted company, and ended by falling into the arms of Brian Pitman's Lloyds Bank. Most of the major UK securities houses and merchant bankers have also lost their independence, usually to foreign buyers. Smith New Court, the UK's leading equity market maker, is now part of Merrill Lynch. Kleinwort Benson, who kicked off the privatisation boom with the BT sale in 1984, is now owned by Dresdner Bank. Hoare Govett has passed into the hands of ABN AMRO, and Barings was rescued, if that's the right word, by ING. But the greatest surprise of all was that the bear market in bonds in 1994 effectively brought down the flagship of the UK securities industry: Warburgs. It emphasised the fragility of the UK securities industry that its leader could be laid low by one bad year. Warburgs was not only a leader in its own right in corporate finance, but it also included some famous names which it had brought together at Big Bang: Rowe & Pitman the corporate finance brokers; Akroyd & Smithers the jobbers; Mullens the government gilt brokers; plus a controlling interest in the UK's premier fund management house, MAM.

The statistics

Apart from the Bank of England's belated impersonation of King Canute, there was little to stop the take-over tide in the 1980s, and virtually nothing now. The net result was a staggering flow of bids and deals which culminated in the failed record-breaking Hoylake £13.4bn bid for BAT in the summer of 1989. The statistics are:

Table 3.1 Mergers and acquisitions – The 1980s (£bn)

	1980	1981	1982	1983	1984	1985	1986	1987	1988	1989	1990
UK* M&A value £bn	1.5	1.1	2.2	2.3	5.5	7.1	14.9	15.3	22.1	26.1	7.9
UK equities: total return %	35.0	13.5	28.9	28.8	31.6	20.6	27.5	8.0	11.6	36.0	-9.7
YOY RPI %	15.1	12.0	5.4	5.3	4.6	5.7	3.7	3.7	6.8	7.7	9.3
Net gearing † %	26	23	25	17	21	21	18	17	18	37	
Average Base Rate %	16.3	13.3	11.9	9.8	9.7	12.3	10.9	9.7	10.1	13.8	14.8
Real interest rate %	1.2	1.3	6.5	4.5	5.1	6.6	7.2	6.0	3.3	6.1	5.5

* *Source*: DTI. Public companies only.

† Combined balance sheets of large UK companies.

The DTI series is not the most comprehensive currently available, but it does go back twenty years and it is the most useful from the point of view of long-term trends.

Table 3.2 Mergers and acquisitions – The 1970s (£bn)

1970	1971	1972	1973	1974	1975	1976	1977	1978	1979
1.1	0.9	2.5	1.3	0.5	0.3	0.4	0.8	1.1	1.7

The previous peak of M&A activity at £2.5bn in 1972 pales into insignificance compared with £26bn in 1989.

Statistics compiled by the magazine *Acquisitions Monthly*, which include private companies, tell the same story of a merger and acquisition boom in the late 1980s. According to them, the 1988 figure for all M&A activity in the UK was £32bn, rising to £52bn in 1989.

Themes

As the tables show, economic growth, the bull market and low interest rates underpinned the huge rise in take-over activity. In addition, it seems that every take-over boom has to have a number of fashionable themes into which companies and institutions can charge herd-like. Even without the benefit of hindsight, many were founded on highly dubious assumptions and were executed more in the heat of the moment than on any prudent assessment of the financial implications.

'One stop' financial shopping

Aside from Big Bang, the liberalisation of financial markets gave rise to the concept of the 'financial supermarket' where the public could purchase everything from mortgages and pensions to home contents insurance and unit trusts. It was this concept that was a major factor in the expansion of British & Commonwealth (B&C) and the rush by insurance companies, building societies and some banks to acquire estate agents in order to produce mortgage and insurance business. The concept was fine on paper, but it ignored one simple and very obvious fact: the clearing banks had been in a position to offer a basket of financial services for years, and had largely failed in their attempts to 'cross-sell' new services to existing customers. Sir Peter Middleton, the Deputy Chairman of Barclays, tells a story which illustrates this problem, about an incident which occurred shortly after he joined Barclays and was touring some branches. He found a group of customers queuing outside a branch to use an auto-teller machine in the rain when the branch's cashier counters were virtually empty. He invited one member of the queue to come inside to use the cashiers. When they got inside and the man had cashed his cheque he expressed relief saying "I thought for one terrible moment you were going to try to sell me some life insurance".

The new generation of financial supermarkets fared little better than the clearers had. Apart from the B&C disaster (see Appendix II), the Prudential and Abbey National were forced to do an embarrassing *volte face* and to sell their estate agency chains, virtually giving them away for losses of hundreds of millions of pounds. Hambros, which deployed the cash it raised from the sale of its stake in Hambro Life (Allied Dunbar as it became) into estate agency at close to the top of the market, is still struggling with the loss-making Hambro Countrywide.

If it's a growth market, we will make money

Investors have consistently lost money by assuming that if they invest in the equity of companies engaged in a growth market it is logical that they must make money. They should take a leaf from the book of US investors in the 1970s who correctly identified air travel as a growth market and then underperformed the market by investing in airline stocks. How? Because they missed the point that the link between growth in air travel and the profitability of airlines was about to be broken by the intervention of a force called deregulation. More air miles were flown, but at lower and lower fares.

Similarly, UK corporates in the 1980s correctly identified trends such as the demography which was making the current middle-aged generation in the UK the first consistently to inherit property from their parents which would give them free capital to invest. Theories such as this spurred the amazing multiples which were paid for fund management operations, such as Hypobank's acquisition of Foreign & Colonial and Bank in Liechtenstein's bid for GT or NatWest's bid for Gartmore on twenty times earnings. On a grander scale, Lloyds Bank acquired Abbey Life and most of the other banks acquired or established their own life insurance operations. What they all missed was the extent to which sales of life policies had been dependent not upon inheritance and demographics, but the housing market which sold endowment policies. And when that collapsed in 1990, so did the life market. To compound the pain, there was then the scandal about the mis-selling of personal pensions.

1992 and all that

The preparations for the single European market in 1992 was another reason to hype the take-over game, although this appeared to afflict those investing in the UK more than the other way around. Indeed, corporate UK, still hamstrung by an inability to speak foreign languages, continued to be besotted more by the United States than by the opportunities in its own backyard. This is shown by the following table:

Table 3.3 Spending on corporate acquisitions into and out of the UK

	1990		1989	
	No.	Value £m	No.	Value £m
UK domestic	1228	14062	1825	29572
UK into EC (excl UK)	279	4522	380	3655
UK into Europe (excl EC)	19	177	30	69
UK into US	167	4998	262	10198
UK into others	69	1326	92	1168
EC (excl UK) into UK	167	5668	122	5165
Europe (excl UK) into UK	31	436	42	1299
US into UK	47	1171	51	9171
Others into UK	51	6341	38	2025

Source: Acquisitions Monthly

Now that 1992 has passed it is easy to see that it has made very little difference. Nevertheless, investors who suffered from Morgan Grenfell's brief quoted existence will have been grateful for the bid in 1989 from Deutsche Bank at 2.3 times book value. However, they were not as grateful as former investors in Equity & Law or Pearl Assurance. The former was taken over by Compagnie du Midi on 54 times earnings, and the latter by AMP (Australian Mutual Provident) on 29 times earnings. Even allowing for the embedded value of the long-term business, both exit multiples were very generous and now look even more so given the recent slowdown in life assurance and pension sales.

And the irony of it all is did 1992 make any difference? None that I can discern. Still it was a good slogan to get a few deals going.

CONGLOMERATES AND UNBUNDLING

The conglomerates have been nearly as acquisitive as ever during the 1990s. BTR found a new lease of life under Australian Alan Jackson and bid for

Hawker Siddeley in 1990. Hanson bought ConsGold and Beazer, swopped gold for forests with Jimmy Goldsmith, bought Quantum Chemical, sold Beazer Homes and US Industries and bought Eastern Electricity. Tomkins out bid Hanson for Rank Hovis McDougall and most recently acquired Gates Rubber in the States.

But the take-over boom of the 1980s reached its high-water mark with a move towards unbundling. Like many of the phrases coined in the 1980s take-over boom, unbundling is an ugly word which sits appropriately alongside other inventions such as the junk bond and greenmail. The phrase can be attributed to Sir James Goldsmith, whose Hoylake consortium including Kerry Packer and Jacob Rothschild planned to unbundle BAT. In the end, BAT partially unbundled itself, selling Argos and Wiggins Appleton. In fact the practice had been perfected as early as 1986 by Lord Hanson with one of the UK's original mega bids, the take-over of Imperial Group. Or was that asset stripping? It's so easy to get confused.

Unbundling proved to be exportable across the Atlantic where it was akin to taking coals to Newcastle. Indeed, Hanson was as adept at unbundling over there as over here, SCM being perhaps the pinnacle of his US achievements. The titanium dioxide interests were retained and the rest of SCM was re-floated. This gave the US market some practice in discovering that things should generally not be bought from Hanson, a lesson which the UK market has recently relearned with Beazer Homes. Then of course, ICI appeared to offer the greatest prize of all, but eluded Hanson.

But herein lies the catch. Growth through continued acquisition is like a drug. The more successful each deal is, the bigger the next deal has to be to make an impact and continue the pattern of growth. This was the seed of some of the creative accounting practices which came to bedevil corporate UK in the late 1980s. The take-over vehicles not only found that bigger and bigger take-overs were necessary to maintain profits growth, but also found a series of techniques associated with acquisitions and disposals which could be used to boost profits.

The final stage in unbundling for Hanson, king of the acquisitive conglomerates, came when it announced its own split into four businesses since it could no longer add value by acquisition.

MBOs and LBOs

With the exception of the £2bn Isosceles deal for which Warburgs earned in the region of £20m in the summer of 1989, mega bids involving buyouts and buyins by a company's management or others were not a major feature of the UK corporate scene in the 1980s to the same extent that they were in the US, where they culminated in KKR's bid for RJR Nabisco, immortalised in the book *Barbarians at the Gate*. Apart from Isosceles, the three major deals involving household names in the UK were Magnet, Lowndes Queensway and Woolworth. Unfortunately, the timing of the first two, at the top of the consumer boom, was to be catastrophic. Both deals were dashed on the rocks of rising interest rates from mid 1988 which led to crippling costs of debt service on the one hand and falling demand for their products on the other. In the end, the banks who advanced the loans for the leverage were left holding the baby. But just to show that the corporate finance market is good at recycling, Magnet has since rejoined the ranks of the stock market by being reversed into Berisford after it was purchased from the long-suffering banks for a song.

The decade was not without some success in the MBO market with the Premier Brands buyout from Cadbury Schweppes standing out in the somewhat safer area of food processing. The Woolworth buyout (originally called Paternoster Stores) succeeded where the other retail MBOs failed – partly because it happened in an earlier stage of the retail cycle, a conclusion which has been reinforced by the difficulty which Kingfisher (as Woolworth has been rechristened) experienced in 1994/95. Timing in this area of M&A activity, as much as anywhere else, is crucial.

Even a brief résumé of the LBO/MBO market in the 1980s would not be complete without mentioning the relatively small management buyout of the commercial service activities of British & Commonwealth by Bricom in June 1988 for £359m. Although B&C retained a 22.5% interest this was effectively the beginning of the end for the group, because it removed most of the tangible assets from the balance sheet, leaving only a highly dubious pile of goodwill relating to the newly acquired financial companies. These proved to be of little support when the Atlantic Computers take-over finally brought the house down. The Bricom buyout was done on an exit PE of 19.6, but there was much hidden value in the various commercial services companies reflecting very conservative accounting policies over the years.

The new owners were quickly able to unlock this value. Over half the acquisition loan was repaid within eighteen months. The 1990 medium-term debt instalment was paid a year early, and in March 1990 the forced sale by B&C of most of its 22.5% stake to other investors was done at a price twice as high as the management buyout. Within a few months the crazy accounting at Atlantic Computers had brought B&C crashing to earth in one of the most dramatic UK corporate failures ever. And, as if to add insult to injury, the debt free Bricom was sold to a Swedish buyer for £338m. It, effectively, was the B&C of the Cayzers. Old money and prudent accounting had survived and prospered despite an initial mountain of debt. The brash financial services conglomerate built with highly-rated paper and supported by what proved to be invisible earnings, was strangled almost at birth.

Hence the saying: What is a definition of a recession? A time when money is returned to its rightful owners. The brash financial services conglomerate with its poorly accounted computer leasing subsidiary was not really a store of wealth. It had just borrowed it from the Cayzers, the founders of B&C, who had introduced John Gunn only to find that his strategy was not to their taste. Their money was promptly returned to them when B&C went bust through the guarantee which Barclays Bank had given for the repayment of the preference shares they took when they left (see Appendix II). How suitable an epitaph for the Decade of the Deal.

It will all be different this time

In 1992 the ending to this chapter was called 'And now the hangover'. It went through the litany of shattered companies and reputations that resulted from the take-over boom of the 1980s. But this no longer seems appropriate since a new take-over boom is upon us, marked by the upsurge in activity in 1995:

Table 3.4   UK takeovers 1990–1995

£bn	1990	1991	1992	1993	1994	1995
UK public companies acquired	10.7	6.2	9.9	3.0	5.1	
UK private companies acquired	6.8	5.9	4.5	5.7	12.5	
UK divestments	10.2	6.0	5.3	8.6	7.2	
	27.7	18.1	19.7	17.3	24.8	67.8

What are the themes of this new take-over boom? The recovery from the recession has been characterised by low growth and low inflation. The net result is that many companies are finding that their automatic ability to increase prices as a method of growing turnover and keeping ahead of rising overheads is gone. The consumer has been fed on a diet of discounting and continuous sales during the recession. Retailers finding themselves squeezed are in turn squeezing their suppliers. This is a natural consequence of a low inflationary environment. How else can low inflation be imposed than through price restraint?

In banking, in contrast to the 1980s, the 1990s have seen a dearth of loan demand as the housing boom has ended and corporate UK and Essex Man have both learnt the downside of debt gearing. This has led to the odd combination of a lack of growth in income, as loans are the main generator of interest and non interest income, and burgeoning capital since there is no growth in loan assets to finance. The result of similar conditions in America, i.e. surplus capital and few opportunities to lend, has been a merger mania amongst the regional banks. After all, if you cannot increase profits by growing income, how about cutting costs? Merging banks and cutting out duplicated branches and head office functions is supposedly a route to this, although that ignores research and common-sense which shows that larger banks are less not more cost efficient. But this has not stopped the US merger mania going beyond the regional banks to encompass the merger of Chemical Bank and Chase Manhattan.

In M&A what happens in America today is the UK's fad of tomorrow. Lloyds has already bid for TSB, and the merger has been hailed by the market as another stroke of genius from Brian Pitman since the new enlarged bank is bound to be more cost efficient. In fact, this was Lloyds' second major acquisition within four months; it had acquired the Cheltenham & Gloucester building society in the summer of 1995. Abbey, the building society which floated in 1989, has bid for the National & Provincial building society, and it would be a brave man, or a foolish fund manager, who would bet that this marks the end of merger mania in the UK's financial sector. Never mind all the research which shows that take-overs rarely deliver value for shareholders, or that larger banks are less cost efficient. In the world of M&A you must never let the facts get in the way of a good story!

Similar pressures have also produced a new wave of take-overs in the pharmaceutical sector in the 1990s. The industry had a good recession, when it proved yet again that spending on healthcare is little affected by economic conditions. But the recovery found it in less good shape. Governments had become alarmed by the inexorable rise of healthcare spending, particularly spending on drugs, as a proportion of GDP, and none more so than in America, the world's biggest healthcare market. This combined with the imminent expiry of some key patents which protect the profitability of drugs, most notably on Glaxo's Zantac, the world's best selling drug. The exact response to this likely slowdown in sales growth has varied slightly, but there are common elements with the response of other sectors, such as the banks, in Glaxo's blockbusting bid for Wellcome which was based on the premise of lowering research costs for the combined group. Other responses were more difficult to fathom.

One response to spiralling drug costs in America was the mushrooming of so-called pharmaceutical benefit managers. These organisations managed healthcare programmes to extract the best purchasing deals for drugs and other services. The drug companies' response was to buy them in a wave of take-overs in 1994-95. How a pharmaceutical benefit manager would fit within a drugs company with whom it was meant to play hard ball in price negotiations was to say the least unclear. It seems a bit like putting the fox in charge of the hen coop, a fact which may not be entirely beyond the grasp of the Federal Trade Commission. But it was clearer than the logic behind the prices paid. SmithKline Beecham paid $2.3bn for Diversified Pharmaceutical Services, a company with operating profits of $39.9m and assets of just $60m. But according to analysts, despite the exit multiple of 88 times historic earnings, the acquisition did not dilute earnings. What is even more amazing is that analysts actually copied this statement down and sent it out to clients under the guise of research.

But events in another sector which has been a take-over theme for the 1990s make those in banking and pharmaceuticals seem almost sane. I refer of course to media. If you have a company into which you can fit the words 'multi media', the world is your oyster. There has been a scramble for terrestrial TV stations in the UK, and groups such as Pearson have decided that they are no longer conglomerates with the *Financial Times*, Lazards, Madame Tussauds, Wedgwood, etc. but media groups, which they went on to demonstrate by buying Thames TV, Grundy Television (makers of the *Neighbours* soap opera), and Mindscape, a maker of cartridge games for computers and CD-ROM. Dorling Kindersley, the publisher of illustrated books, had a period of glory when some of its books were published on CD-ROM by Microsoft, the dominant force in software under Bill Gates, which also took a stake in the company. A soaring share price and M&A deals were the reward for any company which could claim the slightest association with the Internet. Never mind that most investors and other ordinary mortals had no acquaintance with the Internet or multimedia at all, and even those who were involved struggled to find a way to profit from it. It was a growth market, so these deals were bound to make money. Where have I heard that before?

Even the supposedly boring privatised utilities enjoyed their own take-over boom, especially the RECs, which were bid for by US utilities, water companies, conglomerates, other RECs and power generators. No one seemed to stop in the middle of this feeding frenzy to reflect that the take-overs were occurring in the run-up to a General Election which seemed very likely to return a Labour Government – which might have a marked effect on the profitability of these utilities. But then that's a take-over boom for you.

Part II

Accounting Techniques Old and New

4

ACQUISITION ACCOUNTING

'The Black Hole of British accounting'
Sir David Tweedie

The first substantive chapter of the first edition of *Accounting for Growth* dealt with what it called the 'Pre-Acquisition Write-Down' and this second edition starts in exactly the same place. The continuing significance of this subject is given credibility by David Tweedie's view, expressed above.

Why did David Tweedie call this 'the Black Hole of British accounting' and why has there been more ballyhoo about this area of accounting than probably any other? Because UK GAAP allowed a heaven-sent opportunity to an acquisitive company to cook the books. Most accounting regimes require that the assets and liabilities of a company being acquired should be brought into the acquiror's balance sheet at so-called fair value.

What this means in practice is that adjustments are applied to the values of these assets and liabilities to bring the acquired assets and liabilities into line with a) the acquiror's accounting policies, and b) current rather than historic values. Sounds quite logical doesn't it? In common with some other techniques of creative accounting such as writing off goodwill to the balance sheet, it can even be made to sound conservative: "we are writing down the value of the assets we have acquired, applying more stringent accounting treatment and valuations, etc". You can almost hear the finance director preaching. However . . .

Fair value accounting has presented a great opportunity to acquisitive companies. To the extent that they write down the value of current assets such as stock and debtors, whatever profit is later realised from the disposal of these current assets is increased (or losses reduced). If fixed assets are written down, then the future depreciation charge is reduced, so profits are boosted. Profits on disposals of fixed assets could also be boosted. This could leave the curious situation in which a company sold fixed assets at a loss compared with their cost, but above their written down value, and was then allowed to show a profit on the transaction.

But there were two other aspects of fair value accounting which were even more heaven-sent for the acquisitive company looking for a boost to its profits and share price. The first is the reorganisation provision. The acquiring company might need to take action to improve the profitability of its target. Plants need to be closed, work forces slimmed etc, and there are costs associated with these actions in the form of redundancy payments and capital expenditures. Why not therefore recognise these costs at the outset of the acquisition by including reorganisation provisions in the fair value adjustments?

What a great opportunity. These provisions could be retained on the balance sheet, which is the second great opportunity presented by fair value accounting: at least until very recently, the adjustments went to write down the balance sheet value of the assets acquired. There was no damage to the precious profit & loss account. The reorganisation costs were then used to reduce the reorganisation provision on the balance sheet as they are incurred. This was vital in an investment world in which analysts and investors were, and still are, fixated by earnings per share, a performance figure derived from the profit & loss account. The write down of assets even enhanced the ostensible performance for those analysts who took the trouble to calculate return on equity or return on capital since shareholders' funds are reduced by the write downs (see Chapter 16: Goodwill).

'Trust me . . . I'm an acquiror'

And we will trust the company to use these provisions solely to cover costs involved in making the acquired company more efficient. It is of course ludicrous to suggest that companies might sometimes use reorganisation provisions to cover ordinary expenses. Or is it?

Take the example of Trafalgar House's acquisition of Davy Corporation. Davy owned an oil rig, the Emerald Field rig known amongst analysts as 'the curse of Davy' since its construction had brought down Davy Corporation.

Trafalgar House's acquisition of Davy was the last fling of the acquisitive regime of Sir Nigel Broackes before the recession brought down the curtain and resulted in control of Trafalgar House passing to Hongkong Land who struggled unsuccessfully with the legacy of problems. When Hongkong Land gained control it had to make a number of adjustments to the 1991 accounts after the intervention of the Financial Reporting Review Panel, the ASB's 'teeth' for enforcing implementation of standards. A number of these changes are reviewed in Chapter 13 on UITF Abstract 5, for which Trafalgar House is an excellent case study. But the particular adjustment to the 1991 accounts for the Emerald rig is of interest for students of acquisition accounting in the UK:

> *Exhibit 4.1* **Trafalgar House Accounts 1992**
>
> Turnover on continuing business was fractionally down at £3,877m (£3,884m), whilst operating profits, pre-writedowns, declined to £77.5m (£126.8m). *The interest charge rose 47% to £41.7m (£28.3m).*
>
> Trafalgar House accounts, 1992 (*My italics*)

What is the significance of the restatement in Trafalgar House's 1992 accounts leading to an increased interest charge? In 1991 £13m of interest payable in respect of the Emerald rig had been charged to acquisition provisions. Now most people would regard interest payable as an expense which should appear in the profit & loss account, and would not regard covering interest payments with acquisition provisions as a proper use of this technique or likely to enhance the transparency of accounts. So much for trusting people!

Faced with such blatant use (or abuse) of acquisition provisions to enhance reported profits, you can perhaps see why I have always avoided what I regard as the arcane debate amongst analysts about the 'quality' of the use of provisions. In this strange pseudo science, analysts use phrases such as "it's OK, those are provisions with a cash cost" i.e. they are not just asset write downs which could enhance future profits as the assets are sold or the depreciation charge is cut. The fact that provisions are associated with an actual cash cost provides very cold comfort in my view. If an acquiror subsequently incurs cash costs of reorganisation to clear a factory site or make workers redundant, for example, to the extent that provisions are used to cover these costs, which therefore do not appear in the profit & loss account, the result is that profits overstate cash generated by the business, and I am always suspicious when profits do not equal cash.

Never mind the quality, feel the width

My attitude to provisions and acquisitions in general is probably best encapsulated in the name of an old TV sitcom about tailoring: *Never Mind the Quality, Feel the Width*. The only judgements we can make about the quality of acquisition adjustments and provisions involve listening to the management, and in my view they are generally not to be trusted where the matter impacts their share price, and their consequent ability to make further acquisitions and enhance the value of their share options.

I therefore continue to fall back upon the tried and trusted method which I put forward in the first edition of this book, which is to compare the fair value adjustments and provisions with various yardsticks, and if they are big, then so is the potential for management to pull the wool over our eyes.

BTR/Hawker Siddeley

Was acquisition accounting still in use after 1992? In 1990, BTR completed a hostile bid for Hawker Siddeley. There were many reasons to query the logic of this deal. It was a take-over which was missed by many engineering analysts who believed that no one would bid for Hawker Siddeley because it consisted of a large number of diverse businesses, none of which were market leaders. It was a test for the new BTR team of Alan Jackson as Chief Executive and Kathleen O'Donovan, the new Finance Director and formerly with BTR's auditors Ernst & Young. The glory of the previous regime at BTR under Sir Owen Green and Norman Ireland (who had completed the spectacularly successful take-overs of Dunlop and Thomas Tilling), had begun to fade, and BTR had conspicuously failed to gain control of Pilkington in a hostile bid in 1987. Faced with need to 'do a deal', BTR even increased its bid for Hawker Siddeley despite an absence of a competitive bid. It is always dangerous if companies feel they have to do a deal, rather than finding a deal which is so compelling it has to be done.

The immediate aftermath of the bid was an upsurge in support for BTR's shares as the City showed its relief that the acquisitive conglomerate was still able to fulfil its function in life. This was helped by a series of fine results from BTR in which it maintained its legendary high margins on manufacturing which hovered around 15% compared with 10% for most other manufacturers. Results were accompanied by statements that the Hawker Siddeley companies were performing well. And no wonder. Hawker Siddeley cost £1513m and had net assets of £748m. BTR made fair value adjustments of £285m in 1991 and a further £160m in 1992 as permitted by SSAP 22 (revised) and ED53. If the acquiring company's accounts are compiled too soon after the take-over for it to complete the assessment of fair value adjustments, then a provisional assessment could be made with adjustments in the next set of accounts. How did this total of £445m in fair value adjustments compare with other take-overs in terms of size?

When the BTR/Hawker Siddeley deal is slotted into the table comparing fair value adjustments from the 1992 edition of *Accounting for Growth*, it is apparent that it exceeded the proportion of asset value or purchase consideration written off in other major engineering take-overs, with a whopping 60% of Hawker's net asset value written off, and 30% of the purchase price.

Table 4.1 Comparison of fair value adjustments

TI: Crane, Bundy, Thermal Scientific	£m
Book value assets acquired*	270.8
Fair value adjustments	59.3
Fair value adjustments/book value assets (%)	21.9
Fair value adjustments/consideration (%)	**11.0**
Turner & Newall: JPI	
Book value assets acquired	159.5
Fair value adjustments	14.1
Fair value adjustments/book value assets (%)	8.8
Fair value adjustments/consideration (%)	**7.0**
Vickers: Cosworth	
Book value assets acquired	27.1
Fair value adjustments	2.8
Fair value adjustments/book value assets (%)	10.3
Fair value adjustments/consideration (%)	**1.7**
Siebe: Foxboro	
Book value assets acquired	112.5
Fair value adjustments	48.1
Fair value adjustments/book value assets (%)	42.7
Fair value adjustments/consideration (%)	**13.0**
BTR: Hawker Siddeley	
Book value of assets acquired	748.0
Fair value adjustments	445.0
Fair value adjustments/book value assets (%)	59.5
Fair value adjustments/consideration (%)	**29.4**

*Book value of assets acquired on consolidation are not available. These figures have been struck after fair value adjustments.

Moreover, no less than £223m of the fair value adjustments were re-organisation provisions. Hawker Siddeley had been taken over before reporting its 1990 profits, but these were estimated at about £120–125m p.a. It would be difficult not to show some improvement in performance from a company where you had provisions available to cover costs equivalent to twice annual profits.

In late 1993 I began to query BTR's superior margins which had held up well during the recession and the subsequent margin pressures in industry caused by a low inflation economy, and to wonder whether these sustained superior margins were the result of the use of these provisions. That this is not just a case of jobbing backwards is shown by the last paragraph of *The Sunday Times* article on page 7. I met a barrage of criticism from some investors who often told me how well BTR used provisions, that they were used to cover cash costs etc. I kept repeating my litany: never mind the quality, feel the width. It was therefore of less surprise to me than to some others that BTR's margins fell when it reported its profits in 1994, with a catastrophic effect on the share price.

Figure 4.1   BTR share price relative to the All Share Index

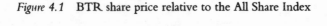

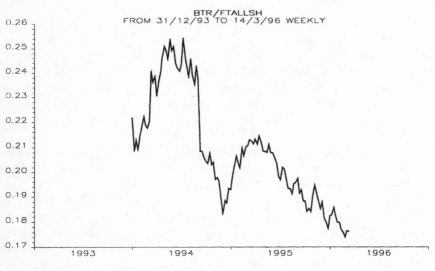

In 1992, BTR had used provisions of £305m (not all of which were for Hawker Siddeley) in reporting pre-tax profits of £1085m. Think about that. One third of reported profits were there only because BTR had provisions with which to cover costs. In the first half of 1993, a further £81m were utilised, of which £47m were for Hawker Siddeley, in reaching profits of £602m. This left £93m of Hawker Siddeley provisions outstanding. It did not require a brain the size of a planet to work out that the Hawker Siddeley provisions would be exhausted in 1994, and that then BTR might struggle to maintain its profitability.

Of course it's all different now

Citing the example of BTR's use of acquisition adjustments is not just an exercise in advanced egomania. It is meant to show that problems in this area persisted long after the publication of the first edition of *Accounting for Growth* and the advent of the ASB. Of course we now have an accounting regime in which reorganisation provisions are placed through the profit & loss account. This certainly makes them more visible. It seems that it is easy for highly paid analysts to find it difficult or too tiring to look in a company's balance sheet! But this is only a partial solution to the problem. The impact of so-called 'big bath' provisions going through the profit and loss account is dealt with in Chapter 7 on FRS 3.

There is a danger that investors will still not be alerted by the fact that provisions are raised through the profit & loss account sufficiently for them to extract the subsequent utilisation of these provisions from the enhancement of future performance. Frankly this is not a problem of accounting disclosure. The ASB has probably done all that it can to bring these fair value adjustments to our attention. What is needed now is that we should do the difficult part and think about them rather than being misled by some companies' smokescreens about the quality of their use of provisions.

Other innovations introduced by the ASB include restrictions on the use of reorganisation provisions, so that, for example, they cannot overtly be raised for purposes such as covering anticipated future trading losses. Not before time. It comes to something when we have to congratulate ourselves on such a blatantly necessary reform. When did you ever see a company raise an asset for anticipated future trading profits? I always find it instructive in judging fine sounding phrases to see whether they make sense when they are reversed like this; for example, the UK bank whose explanation for its costs rising faster than income is that it was 'investing for the future'. Have you come across any examples of companies investing for the past?

As you will gauge, as long as companies are able to make fair value adjustments and reorganisation provisions in any form, I suspect investors' only protection will remain the sort of calculations which are shown for BTR.

5

SALES AND DISPOSALS

Man proposes but God disposes
Thomas à Kempis

No more trouble with disposals?

Developments in UK accounting have made the original chapter on Disposals largely redundant. It showed the large number of different ways in which companies disclosed disposal profits. Some of the commonest problems occurred with industries which customarily experience property disposals – not just the property companies, but also for example the multiple retailers, whose branch networks were constantly changing.

There was always a desire to show these disposal profits 'above the line' i.e. the attributable profit line at which earnings per share were calculated, and not as an extraordinary item 'below the line'. Unless of course a loss was incurred, in which event this desire was automatically reversed. But once a disposal profit had been successfully shifted above the line, a subsidiary debate then ensued. Should it be shown as an exceptional item? This risked the analytical community identifying it (not even investment analysts are usually capable of missing items in the accounts which are separately identified on the face of the profit and loss account) and so excluding it from the measure of ongoing or sustainable earnings to which a PE is attached – much to the chagrin of the management who naturally wanted these disposal profits included in the profits to which the PE was applied in order to inflate the value of the company.

Even more fun and games could be had when disposals of companies rather than individual assets were involved. But FRS 3 put paid to most of these manoeuvres. By effectively banishing extraordinary items it took away at a stroke the incentive for managements to strive in order to get a disposal profit shown 'above the line'.

SELLING A BUSINESS

Another area of clear improvement since 1992 is UITF Abstract 3 on the

34

'Treatment of goodwill on disposal of a business', which stopped groups selling businesses and showing the profit or loss compared with the written down value. Almost invariably, write downs had been taken to the balance sheet value when the business was acquired, so that the company could show a profit on disposal when the sales proceeds were compared with the written down value. Thus, a company could buy a subsidiary for £500m. If the fair value of the assets acquired was estimated at £150m, goodwill of £350m would be written off, leaving the value of the subsidiary's net assets as £150m. If it was then sold for £400m, prior to UITF Abstract 3, the group could show a profit on the sale of £250m. UITF Abstract 3 forced the company to take the cost before the write down into account when reporting whether there had been a profit or loss on disposal. A good example is shown in the adjustments to Trafalgar House's 1991 profits on page 117 in chapter 13 on Transfers from Current to Fixed Assets.

This simply brought the accounting rules relating to disposals of businesses into line with common sense. I would look at whether I had made a profit or loss on selling my house by comparing the sale price with the cost, not with the last estimated value of the house, which would almost invariably not be the price I had paid for it.

SELLING ASSETS

But just to continue the traditional confusion which seems to surround accounting for disposals, a seemingly contradictory stance is dictated by FRS 3 for the reporting of disposals of assets:

Exhibit 5.1   **Queens Moat Houses 1992 Annual Report**

Profit on disposals of fixed assets. Previously, profits and losses arising on the disposal of fixed assets carried at valuation were included in the profit and loss account based upon the difference between the sale proceeds and depreciated historical cost. In accordance with the requirements of FRS 3, this policy has been changed and such profits and losses are now included based upon the difference between the sales proceeds and the net carrying amount, whether at valuation or at depreciated historical cost. This restatement reduces pre-tax profits in 1991 by £24.2m.

So although there has been clear progress since 1992, there are still some grey areas. And within those grey areas lurk the opportunities to simmer the books.

DECONSOLIDATION ON DISPOSAL

An option available to companies is to *deconsolidate* from their group results a subsidiary at the time when they decide to sell it rather than when a sale is completed. The profits (or more likely the losses) of the subsidiary between the announcement and completion are added to the profit or loss on disposal. This technique has the major advantage of keeping the results of a loss-making subsidiary out of the profit & loss account.

TSB/Target Deconsolidation

Table 5.1   TSB 1990 interim results – Deconsolidation of Target

	1990 £m	1989 £m	% change
Reported Pre-tax Profits	175	164	+7
Target Group*	(17)	3	
Restated TSB Results	158	167	–5

*Not consolidated because decision taken to dispose of Target

---

Exhibit 5.2   TSB Interims announcement to 30 April 1990

Target Group
The results for Target Group for the half year to 30 April 1990 have not been consolidated as the decision to dispose of the business was taken early in the period. The results of Target Group in the relevant periods were:

	Half year to 30 April 1990	Half year to 30 April 1989	Half year to 31 October 1989
Pre-tax (loss)/profit	(17)	3	3

The results for the period include a reduction in the embedded value of the life and pensions business in force of some £15m due mainly to changes in taxation and more conservative assumptions on lapse rates. They also include provisions for likely ex-gratia payments to clients of Garston Amhurst together with associated costs.

In the full year results, the loss for the period to date will be included in the extraordinary profit or loss on disposal.

The Group's investment in Target Group is included in 'other accounts receivable' in the amount of £55m.

TSB took the decision to dispose of its interest in the life assurance and fund management group Target, early in its 1989/90 financial year. When it published its results for the half year to April 90, it did not consolidate the Target Group results and included its £55m investment in Target as 'other accounts receivable' in the TSB balance sheet.

Target reported a pre-tax loss of £17m for the first half of 1989/90 against a profit of £3m in the comparable period. Had this result been consolidated in TSB's interim figures, the pre-tax profits would have shown a decline of five per cent rather than the seven per cent growth reported (see Table 5.1). A useful contribution at a time when TSB was under pressure because of its poor performance post flotation. TSB still had not sold Target at its year end (October 1990).

Midland/EAB – taking deconsolidation a stage further

Midland's disastrous foray into Californian banking in the 1980s through Crocker National Bank is now infamous. But prior to this direct entry into international banking, Midland's overseas representation was via a number of so-called consortium banks – banks which have a group of other banks as their shareholders. In New York, Midland had a 15 per cent shareholding in a consortium bank called European American Bancorp (EAB).

Midland was required to reduce its shareholding in EAB when it bought Crocker because of the then US laws restricting inter-state banking. So the approval for the Crocker acquisition given by the Federal Reserve Board in 1981 required Midland to reduce its stake in EAB to five per cent or less. But this became urgent in 1983–84 for other reasons: in 1983 Crocker lost £17m before tax and in 1984 this soared to £222m reducing Midland Group pre-tax profit from £251m in 1982 to just £135m in 1984. The dividend of £58m was uncovered. But when things go wrong, they rarely go wrong in just one place, especially in banking. In 1984 EAB made a loss net of tax of £133m, of which Midland's share was some £20m.

From the time of the Federal Reserve approval in 1981, Midland continued to treat its holding in EAB as an associate company, even though the holding was below the 20 per cent level which is normally required for an associate treatment by the definition contained in SSAP1, since Midland's EAB holding qualified as an associate on another part of the SSAP1 definition, that of 'significant' influence since Midland had a representative on EAB's Board. As a result, Midland took into its profit and loss account its share of EAB's profits.

Suddenly, in 1984, Midland reduced its representation on EAB's Board and redefined the holding from an associate company to a trade investment

Exhibit 5.3 **Midland 1984 Accounts**

27. Trade Investments

At cost less provisions	Book amount	Valuation 1984	Book amount	Valuation 1983
Group				
Listed elsewhere in Great Britain	1	1	3	3
Unlisted	59	72	23	36
	60	73	25	38
Midland Bank plc				
Unlisted	47	58	13	26

Listed investments are valued at middle market prices and unlisted investments at Directors' valuation.

The principal trade investments at 31 December 1984, all of which were held directly by Midland Bank plc, were as follows

	Country of incorporation	Interest of Midland Bank plc
The Agricultural Mortgage Corporation Limited		
Issued share capital £8.5m	Great Britain	13%
The Bankers' Clearing House Limited		
Issued share capital £1.5m	Great Britain	17%
European American Bancorp		
Issued share capital US$70m	USA	20%
European Banking Company Limited		
Issued share capital £12.2m	Great Britain	14%
European Banking Company SA		
Issued share capital BFrs 3,500m	Belgium	14%
Euro-Pacific Finance Corporation Limited		
Issued share capital A$ 12.5m	Australia	15%

Under the terms of approval given by the Board of Governors of the Federal Reserve Board dated 25 August 1981 to the Midland Bank plc application to acquire a majority interest in Crocker National Corporation it was necessary for the Interest in European American Bancorp (EAB) to be reduced to not more than 5% by October 1984, now extended to 15 October 1985. Midland Bank plc has reduced its representation on the Board of EAB and has treated its holding in EAB as a trade investment rather than an associated company from 1 January 1984. As a trade investment, EAB is stated in the accounts at £35m, after an extraordinary write-down of £6m. The share capital and reserves of EAB at 31 December 1984 amounted for 1984 to US$ 133m.

Exhibit 5.4   **Midland – Consolidated Profit and Loss Account**

Year ended 31 December 1984	Notes	1984 £m	1983 £m
Profit before taxation			
Group excluding Crocker National Corporation		357	242
Crocker National Corporation	11	(222)	(17)
		135	225
Taxation	12	160	100
(Loss) profit after taxation		(25)	125
Minority interests		87	(7)
Profit before extraordinary items	62	118	
Extraordinary items	13	(17)	(4)
Profit attributable to members of Midland Bank PLC		45	114
Dividends	14	58	58
(Deficit) retained profit		(13)	56
Reserves at 1 January		1,396	1,269
Effect of Finance Act 1984 tax changes	12	(230)	0
Other movements in reserves	22	25	71
Reserves at 31 December		1,178	1,396
Earnings per share	15	27.1p	60.6p

The results for Crocker National Corporation, which are after charging £456m (1983 £120m) for bad and doubtful debts, include a profit arising from the disposal of the freehold headquarters buildings amounting to £134m (1983 Nil).

in the 1984 Accounts. What did this rather obscure change of nomenclature achieve? If EAB had remained as an associate, Midland would have been forced to show a £20m loss in its own profit and loss account to reflect EAB's performance. But for the trade investments only any dividend paid is taken to the profit and loss account. EAB's loss was reflected in Midland's accounts as a fall in the value of its trade investment taken to reserves – i.e. it appeared in the balance sheet, not the profit and loss account.

Once again, the profit and loss account escaped unscathed, and the balance sheet suffered.

FRS2 has restricted companies' ability to play fast and loose with the use of deconsolidation. Companies are now restricted to deconsolidating subsidiaries which had not previously been included in the group accounts. That is, a group may decide at the outset of an acquisition if there is a company within the group it acquires that it does not intend to retain. This prevents the sort of convenient "change of heart" which we saw for TSB and Midland at a time when a subsidiary moves into losses. The group must also "reasonably expect" to be able to sell the deconsolidated subsidiary within one year.

This is certainly an improvement, but the technique is still in use even as restricted by FRS 2.

Richmond Power Enterprise was a subsidiary of Hawker Siddeley which BTR decided to sell when it acquired Hawker. It had won power station

---

Exhibit 5.5 BTR Report and Accounts 1991

Richmond Power Enterprise, the unconsolidated 90.5% subsidiary of Hawker Siddeley Group PLC, is held exclusively for resale. The net assets of the company at 31st December 1991 comprise gross assets of £65 million and limited recourse net bank borrowing of £63 million.

---

contracts in America but was making losses. There is no doubt that FRS 2 is an improvement, and that BTR's treatment of Richmond Power Enterprise complied with it: Richmond was sold before BTR's year end. But what I object to is the lack of symmetry in the application of deconsolidation. How often do you see a profitable subsidiary deconsolidated? It does happen, but not very often.

There is little doubt that deconsolidations of loss-making subsidiaries far outweigh deconsolidation of the profitable operations which are for sale. I wonder why?

Q. When is a disposal not a disposal?
A. When you haven't sold anything.

One of the potential problems with disposals which is mentioned in chapter 9 on Contingent Liabilities concerns disposals which bring with them some sort of residual liability. Chapter 9 uses the example of Coloroll's 'disposal' of interests it acquired as part of the John Crowther acquisition to the Response Group MBO, and the sale of Homfray Carpets. In one case, Coloroll sold the securities which it obtained as part of the MBO, but only 'with recourse' (in other words the purchaser had the right to force Coloroll to repurchase them), and in the case of Homfray it retained contingent liabilities by for example guaranteeing the banking facilities used by the purchaser to acquire the businesses.

Apart from the contingent liabilities which Coloroll assumed by the way it engineered these disposals, which became very real when the businesses sold got into difficulty, there is a more direct question to ask. Would anyone using common-sense rather than UK GAAP accounting consider that Coloroll had sold these businesses at all? Probably not, given that Coloroll retained most of the risks of ownership.

SALES

You might think that sales turnover is a relatively uncontroversial area of accounts, whereas it is obvious that disposals of businesses, fixed assets and other exceptional disposals have been a minefield. You would be wrong. Sales are vital. Sales revenue is the income component of the profit equation, and sometimes companies will go to extraordinary lengths to 'create' sales.

A good example of this is provided by Queens Moat Houses:

At its peak, sixty-five of Queens Moat's 103 British hotels were covered by this 'incentive scheme' under which a manager agreed an incentive fee

---

Exhibit 5.6   **Queens Moat Houses 1992 Annual Report**

Licence fees. The group had previously recognised the full fees to be earned in respect of so-called "incentive fee" or licence arrangements with its hoteliers, regardless of the fact that the fee had only been partially paid and the contract covered a period beyond the end of the accounting period. These accounts are prepared on the basis that incentive fees are time apportioned and only that part of the fee relating to the accounting year in question is recognised as income. Your board believes that this is prudent and appropriate to the business. It has resulted, among other things, in reduction in net assets by £48.6 million and pre-tax profits by £13.5m.

---

payable to Queens Moat instead of remitting the revenues from the hotel. Once the fee was agreed, the managers of the hotels each signed a promissory note guaranteeing to pay the fee to Queens Moat in thirteen four-weekly instalments. The incentive to the manager was that he could keep any money the hotel earned over and above the incentive fee as his own profit. The advantage for Queens Moat was that it appeared to guarantee a portion of the annual sales and profits: managers were required to make up any shortfall from their own resources. But problems arose when the company started pushing managers to agree higher and higher incentive fee promissory notes, which were then included in sales and profits even though actual turnover at the hotels was falling as a result of the recession and the Gulf War. Since trading conditions had deteriorated, most of the managers could not make up the shortfall, and in order to try to bridge the gap between reported sales based upon the incentive fees and actual, Queens

Moat would have been faced with the unrealistic alternative of instituting recovery proceedings for these debts against some of its managers.

Moreover, as the notes in the 1992 accounts make clear, Queens Moat had already begun to use the scheme to bring sales and 'profits' forward, by persuading the auditors to allow them to include the fees in sales for the period when the notes were signed rather than the period to which the notes related. How this squares with accrual accounting is beyond me. Accrual accounting is the usual method used in the UK. It involves accruing that part of an income or expense item to the accounts for the period to which it relates. For example, if a company has a long-term contract stretching over several accounting periods, it would obviously distort its reported profits if all of the profit on the contract was reported in the year when it was completed and the cash was received. Instead some part of the estimated profit is attributed to each period, for example, in proportion to the amount of the contract finished in that period. Fairly obviously, if a hotel manager signs a promissory note covering his agreed fees for say two years, it would not be right to include the whole amount in the year he signs.

As a result of the removal of these licence fees from the 1991 figures when they were restated in 1992, sales were reduced by £48.6m and profits by £13.5m. The total impact of all the prior year adjustments to bring Queens Moat's accounts into line with reality was a reduction in sales from £543.3m to £314.7m, a mere 42%.

Exhibit 5.7 **Queens Moat Houses Annual Report & Accounts 1992**

	As previously reported £m	Prior year adjustments £m	Reclassi- fications £m	As restated £m
Turnover	543.3	(230.6)	2.0	314.7
Net operating costs	(385.6)	138.0	(3.7)	(251.3)
Trading profit	157.7	(92.6)	(1.7)	63.4
Rents payable	(9.6)	3.3	-	(6.3)
Depreciation	(1.4)	(33.3)	-	(34.7)
Operating profit	146.7	(122.6)	(1.7)	22.4
Other income	10.8	-	-	10.8
Profit on ordinary activities before interest	157.5	(122.6)	(1.7)	33.2
Interest payable	(67.1)	(22.4)	-	(89.5)
Profit/(loss) on ordinary activities before taxation	90.4	(145.0)	(1.7)	(56.3)
Taxation	(12.3)	(1.9)	1.7	(12.5)
Profit/(loss) for the financial year	78.1	(146.9)	-	(68.8)
Dividends	(33.7)	-	-	(33.7)
Retained profit/(loss) for the year	44.4	(146.9)	-	(102.5)
Other movements	(23.2)	25.3	-	2.1
Profit and loss account at 1 January 1991	129.8	(119.4)	-	10.4
Profit and loss account at 31 December 1991	151.0	(241.0)	-	(90.0)
Earnings/(loss) per share	7.8p			(8.5)p

6

DEFERRED CONSIDERATION

Delays have dangerous ends
Henry VI, Part I (III.ii.33)

Deferred consideration is a payment, the value of which is contingent upon the future performance of the business acquired. More commonly known as 'earn-outs' (from the point of view of the vendors of the business acquired) this technique became popular in structuring acquisitions in the 1980s, particularly for companies within the FT-Actuaries Agencies Sector comprising mainly advertising agencies (this sector ceased to exist from the end of 1990 which gives some indication of the impact of the technique).

Typically in an earn-out the acquiring company would make an up-front payment with further payments in either cash or shares based on a multiple of future profits of the acquired company. This method of acquisition has a number of advantages.

1. Limited downside risk – if the acquisition performs badly, the future deferred consideration payments could be adjusted downwards accordingly.
2. In the 'people' businesses of the Agencies sector, in particular, tying-in the vendors of a business is important as the success of the business often depends heavily upon their creative talents and most of these companies have few tangible assets to rely upon.
3. There was often an immediate enhancement to earnings as the profits of the acquired company were consolidated at once, but the additional consideration was only paid some time later.

But problems can arise. These relate to the ability of the acquiror to finance the future deferred consideration payments, if they are in cash, to the dilutive effect of the shares to be issued and to the resulting cost of maintaining the dividend payment.

It is usual to disclose these potential liabilities rather than providing for them, as the amount is uncertain. An example is Saatchi & Saatchi's 1989 accounts which had contingent liabilities for deferred consideration payments of a maximum of £119.5m (Exhibit 6.1).

Exhibit 6.1 *Saatchi & Saatchi 1989 Accounts*

18. Commitments and Authorisations not provided

Additional capital payments may be made to the vendors of acquired companies in the years to 1995. Such payments are contingent on the future levels of profits achieved by these companies. The Directors estimate that, at the rates of exchange ruling at 30 September 1989, the maximum payments that may be made are as follows:

	£m
Within one year	26.0
From two to five years	92.2
After five years	1.2
	119.5

At 30 September 1989, the Group had the following other commitments in respect of capital expenditure and non-cancellable operating leases for the following year:

	1989 £m	1988 £m
CAPITAL EXPENDITURE		
Committed but not provided for	1.3	3.1
Authorised but not contracted for	5.1	4.9
	6.4	8.0

	Land and buildings £m	Other £m	Total £m
OPERATING LEASES which expire:			
Within one year	5.4	1.6	7.0
From two to five years	14.4	3.0	17.4
Over five years	20.8	0.4	21.2
	40.6	5.0	45.6

The Group balance sheet at the end of 1989 already showed negative net worth of £264.2m after deducting £434.6m goodwill, and this would have been increased significantly by the payment of the deferred consideration, as well as increasing its gearing, with bank loans and overdraft already standing at £121.5m.

Neither are all these problems overcome if the deferred consideration is payable in shares. If the share price of the acquired group is depressed at the time of payment, the result is often the need to issue a greater number of shares in order to fulfil the deferred consideration obligations, which has a highly dilutive effect on Earnings per Share and increases the cost of the total dividend often to a level where the dividend per share must be cut or passed in its entirety, as it was at WPP:

WPP– Deferred consideration commitments

WPP made over 30 small acquisitions by earn-outs, and in 1990 had a total maximum of further payments of around £130m. The payment schedule looks like this (WPP estimates assuming 15 per cent post-tax profits growth):

Table 6.1   WPP – Deferred consideration commitments

	1991	1992	1993	1994	1995	Total
Shares £m	12	6	17	12	2	**49**
Cash £m	19	10	33	17	3	82

Source: WPP

WPP's share price has fallen dramatically due to trading difficulties, caused by the downturn in advertising spend during the recession and the cost of acquisitions, most notably Ogilvy and Mather. With the share price at about 48p in early 1992, against 700p at the beginning of 1990, there was a substantial impact on the future number of shares to be issued:

$$£49m \text{ shares at } 700p = 7.0 \text{ million shares}$$
$$£49m \text{ shares at } 48p = 102.0 \text{ million shares}$$

The company had 43 million shares in issue at the beginning of 1992 – so assuming that these earn-out targets were met, when the share price was 48p, the number of shares in issue would have to be increased nearly 2½ times to meet these commitments. The result was potentially devastating dilution of earnings per share and the impossibility of paying a maintained dividend on the enlarged share capital.

WPP's performance was obviously affected by a number of factors other than its deferred consideration commitments: the recession, Gulf War, the Ogilvy & Mather acquisition and attendant property write-offs. The ordinary dividend was passed in 1990, and the convertible preference dividend in 1991.

Whilst the Saatchi & Saatchi Accounts show the details of the cash deferred consideration commitment in the Note to the Accounts which is

Exhibit 6.2 **Saatchi & Saatchi 1989 Accounts**

13. Creditors

	GROUP 1989		GROUP 1988		COMPANY 1989		COMPANY 1988	
	Due within one yr £m	Due after one yr £m	Due within one yr £m	Due after one yr £m	Due within one yr £m	Due after one yr £m	Due within one yr £m	Due after one yr £m
Loan stock	-	6.2	-	6.3	-	6.2	-	6.3
Bank loans and overdrafts	107.1	121.5	7.4	109.4	93.1	60.0	45.0	-
Trade creditors	499.5	-	461.1	-	-	-	-	-
Subsidiaries	-	-	-	-	281.5	-	276.9	-
Related companies	8.5	0.7	9.2	-	-	-	-	-
Deferred purchase consideration	0.6	1.4	9.4	-	-	-	2.8	-
Finance leases	1.9	2.8	1.6	2.4	-	-	-	-
Taxation and social security	51.2	48.0	49.4	34.2	4.8	-	8.9	-
Other creditors	227.2	32.5	180.4	11.9	3.9	-	2.2	-
Proposed dividends	8.1	-	19	-	5.6	-	16.6	-
	904.1	213.1	737.7	164.2	388.9	66.2	352.4	6.3

The loan stock is convertible and unsecured. It bears interest at 6% and is repayable in 2015 unless previously converted into Ordinary shares. Conversion into Ordinary shares may take place at the option of the Loan stockholders during a specified period in the years to 2015 at £2.465 nominal of Ordinary shares for every £100 nominal of Loan stock. An amount of £6.3 million (1988 – £4.6 million) included in bank loans and overdrafts is secured by mortgages on property.

	GROUP		COMPANY	
Analysis of bank loans and overdrafts by years of repayment	1989 £m	1988 £m	1989 £m	1988 £m
From one to five years	2.6	0.6	-	-
From two to five years	118.7	107.4	60.0	-
Over five years	0.2	1.4	-	-
	121.5	109.4	60.0	-

Gross obligations under finance leases due after more than one year	1989 £m	1988 £m
From two to five years	3.4	3.0
Less future finance charges	0.6	0.6
	2.8	2.4

Exhibit 6.3   WPP 1990 Accounts

21b. Contingent Liabilities – Acquisitions

Acquisitions made in 1990 together with earlier acquisitions (excluding JWT Group, Inc and the Ogilvy Group, Inc) may give rise to further consideration resulting in goodwill, in addition to the initial payments referred to above. Any further payments will be payable in cash and Ordinary shares of the Company dependent upon the level of profitability of these acquired entities over various periods up to 31 December 1995. It is not practicable to estimate with any reasonable degree of certainty the total additional consideration to be paid. However, the directors estimate that the maximum additional payments which may be payable in respect of all subsidiary undertakings, including amounts accrued in the balance sheet at 31 December 1990, would be:

		Payable in	
	Shares	Cash	Total
	£000	£000	£000
Within one year from 31 December 1990	12,951	26,307	39,258
Within two to five years	35,978	35,278	71,256
	48,929	61,585	110,514

The above analysis assumes that the vendors choose cash rather than shares where the option exists. The analysis also assumes that the Company issues shares where the option exists, although in many cases it has the right to settle with cash if it so wishes. Consideration received as shares must generally be retained by the vendors for a minimum period of three years.

---

usually designed to cover capital expenditure authorised and/or contracted, Cray Electronic Holdings disclosed under Note 20 – 'Share Capital' – the maximum deferred consideration commitments for ten acquisitions requiring a maximum of £17.1m which at 67p per share (the price in early 1992) would require an issue of 25.5m shares at Cray's option against 87.4m already in issue.

Marketing services group FKB Group was pushed into administration by these commitments. Note 25 of the 1989 accounts shows a maximum liability for deferred consideration of £58.8m in comparison with shareholders' funds of just £4.7m, after deduction of goodwill on previous acquisitions of £40.1m.

Figure 6.1 WPP share price chart 1985-92

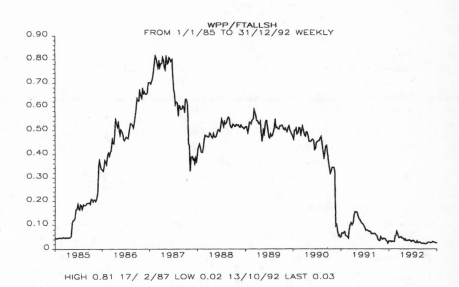

<table>
<tr><td colspan="2" align="center">*Exhibit 6.5* **FKB Accounts to 31 March 1989**</td></tr>
</table>

25. FINANCIAL COMMITMENTS

Additional payments may be made to the vendors of certain acquired companies in the years to 1993. These payments are contingent on the future profits of the respective companies. It is not practicable to estimate with any reasonable degree of certainty the total additional consideration to be paid. However, the Directors estimate that the maximum payments that may be made, using the rates of exchange ruling at 31 March 1989, are as follows:

	£000
Within one year	3,400
Between two and five years	55,400
	58,800

7

FRS 3

Plus ça change, plus c'est la même chose
Alphonse Karr

FRS 3 has probably been the most eagerly awaited of the ASB's reforms to date. Apart from the fact that it changed the appearance and substance of the profit & loss account, the primary instrument through which companies report their performance, it also marked the effective end of the ubiquitous and hence inappropriately named extraordinary item. The conditions for use of extraordinary items in the original ASB Exposure Draft published in 1991 were so restrictive as to make it practically impossible to use them, limiting them to expropriation or confiscation of company assets by a government or a fundamental change in the basis of taxation. But even these relatively rare instances when extraordinary items were acceptable were dropped from FRS 3, and the UITF had already ruled against the use of extraordinary items for redundancy or reorganisation costs.

However, before either describing the interesting features about FRS 3, or the way companies have used it, it may be as well to examine the Standard which it replaced, SSAP6 which governed the use of extraordinary and exceptional items and had gained a very bad name. Why?

ABOVE OR BELOW THE LINE?

SSAP6 covered items over which some of the most frequent debates in accounting raged: extraordinary and exceptional items. Never more than in this area does a conversation between accountants and financial analysts sound more like a debate on linguistic philosophy. So why all the heat and lack of light created by these items?

The answer lies in Earnings per Share (EPS). EPS is usually taken as the single biggest determinant of a share's value, through the ubiquitous Price/Earnings Ratio (PER).

'At 8.15 each weekday morning the security salesmen and analysts at my firm meet to consider the ideas that will be put to our 300 or so institutional customers during the day. Analysts give their recommendations for specific shares: buy, hold or sell. It is these recommendations together with similar conclusions reached at twenty or so other security houses, that collectively drive the share prices in the market. The single most important figure affecting the analysts' and hence the market's view is forecast earnings per share'. (Ian Hay Davison, then Chairman of Alexanders Laing & Cruickshank).

Since EPS is normally calculated by taking earnings before extraordinary items there was a keen interest in deciding whether an item is an exceptional item taken 'above the line' and therefore included in the EPS calculation ('the line' being the line in the profit and loss account at which EPS is calculated) or an extraordinary item taken 'below the line'. This interest increased exponentially if the item was a debit item. Incidentally, for those interested in records, the phrase 'above the line (below the line)' is probably one of the most frequently used/least understood in financial analysis (although 'dilution' runs it a close second).

All this seems surprising given that SSAP6 (revised) gave some apparently clear definitions:

Extraordinary items: are material items which derive from events or transactions that fall outside the ordinary activities of the company and which are therefore expected not to recur frequently or regularly.

Exceptional items: are material items which derive from events or transactions which fall within the ordinary activities of the company, and which need to be disclosed separately by virtue of their size or incidence if the financial statements are to give a true and fair view. (See Table 7.1)

Table 7.1 Examples of exceptional and extraordinary items SSAP6 (revised paras 2 and 4)

	Exceptional	*Extraordinary*
Rationalisation, the reorganisation and redundancy costs	costs relating to continuing business segments	costs arising from discontinuance of a business segment, either through termination or disposal
Fixed assets	profits/losses on disposals arising from an exceptional event	profits/losses on disposals arising from an extraordinary event

	Exceptional	*Extraordinary*
	previously capitalised expenditure on intangible fixed assets written off other than part of a process of amortisation	provisions for a permanent diminution in value of fixed assets (including invetments), because of an extraordinary event
		profits/losses arising from expropriation of assets
		profits/losses arising from the sale of an investment not held for resale, such as investments in subsidiaries and associates
Employee share schemes	amounts transferred to employee share schemes	
Bad debts	abnormal bad debt charges	
Stocks and long-term	abnormal write-offs of contracts stocks or provisions for losses on long-term contracts	
Insurance claims	surpluses arising on the settlement of insurance claims; amounts received in settlement of insurance claims for consequential loss of profits	
Taxation		effect of a change in the basis of taxation or a significant change in Government fiscal policy

Clear enough? But if this is clear, how could the following differences arise:

Exhibit 7.1   **Reckitt & Colman Accounts for 1988**

7. EXTRAORDINARY ITEMS	1988	1987
	£m	£m
Extraordinary income:		
Surplus on disposal of businesses and major sites	15.84	19.45
Extraordinary charges:		
Reorganisation and integration costs of newly		
acquired businesses	(11.86)	(9.51)
	3.98	9.94
Tax relief	3.76	6.19
	7.74	16.13

Reckitt & Colman's 1988 Accounts show an extraordinary gain which includes profits from disposal of businesses and major sites (Note 7), whereas British Aerospace's 1989 Accounts show an exceptional items profit on the sale of the shares in Daf NV and Istel Holdings Ltd (Note 8) even though Daf was an associate company.

Exhibit 7.2   ***British Aerospace 1990 Accounts***

EXCEPTIONAL ITEMS	1990	1989
	£m	£m
Costs associated with industrial action	(28)	(28)
Profit on sale of investments	4	68
	(24)	40

There is no tax charge arising on the profit on sale of investments

Some companies seemed to report extraordinary items with anything other than extraordinary frequency. Table 7.2 below shows the use of extraordinary items to cover closure costs for RHM (Ranks Hovis McDougall) over eight years:

Table 7.2 RHM – Extraordinary closure costs

£m	1984	1985	1986	1987	1988	1989	1990	1991
Extraordinary Closure Costs	14	15	12	20	21	14	24	11
Post tax profits	45	44	59	74	105	125	93	105
Ratio %	31	34	20	27	20	11	26	10

As can be seen, extraordinary closure costs have averaged over 22% of reported net profits over this period. A common-sense approach would suggest that this use of the word 'extraordinary' strains the English language, if not SSAP6.

Why have I taken you on this journey through the history of a now defunct Standard? Because the important feature to note about SSAP 6 is not that it was necessarily a bad Standard. It may have allowed too much latitude for managements to decide whether items should be taken above or below the line. But it was clear enough on some matters, as you can see from the sample text taken from SSAP 6 defining the sale of subsidiaries or associates as extraordinary items, which was completely disregarded by, for example, British Aerospace in accounting for its sale of the Daf stake. The problem was not necessarily with the Standard, but with the unwillingness of some auditors to qualify the accounts of client companies which failed to comply with it, or of the various bodies responsible for accounting over the years to enforce implementation. As a result, before we become too cock-a-hoop about any new Standards, such as FRS 3, we must first see how they are observed.

The profit & loss account format under FRS 3 does for example enable companies to split their reported results between Continuing and Discontinued operations. Obviously, this could present another opportunity for companies to place the inconvenient results of poorly performing or loss-making operations in the Discontinued line in order then to suggest to analysts that the results in this line should be disregarded and the company valued solely on the earnings of its better Continuing operations.

However, FRS 3 contains some very strict criteria for judging whether an operation may be accounted for and described as Discontinued. For example, if an operation is described as Discontinued because it is for sale or closure, this must occur before the earlier of three months into the next financial year or the date on which the accounts are approved.

'BIG BATH' PROVISIONS

Whilst FRS 7 has now dealt with some of the abuses relating to provisions raised in respect of acquisitions, companies are still able to raise reorganisation provisions for ongoing businesses. One of the concerns about this is that these provisions will be disregarded by analysts in the year in which they are raised since they are obviously exceptional items: analysts will 'look through' them and evaluate the company on the basis of its ongoing operating profit before provisions. Therefore the company's rating will not suffer from the reduction in profits caused when the provisions are raised. But it may still gain when the provisions are utilised, either because efficiency is improved or simply because the provisions are used to cover costs. Or they may be released if they are not required.

The fear that companies will be able to divert analysts' attention away from provisioning is oddly at its greatest when the provisions are large, because they cause such a distortion to reported profits when they are raised that analysts are forced to ignore them when attempting to value the shares. These are the so-called 'big bath' or 'kitchen sink' provisions about which the ASB has complained, and they could represent a device for shifting profits from the present into the future without affecting the current share price and to the benefit of the future apparent performance.

Take the example of Grand Met. In 1993, it raised restructuring provisions of £175m for reorganisation of Green Giant and Pearle. Together with a property write down this reduced operating profits from £1,042m to £817m. A further £272m was raised in 1994 for restructuring of Drinks and European Foods which reduced operating profits from £1,023m to £751m. That the focus of concern over provisioning may have shifted from acquisitions to reorganisations of existing businesses is shown by the fact that in 1995 Grand Met raised reorganisation provisions of £122m for its PET acquisition, which represented only 7% of the price paid for PET. This would therefore pass muster on the 'never mind the quality feel the width' test proposed in Chapter 4. But there is no such test which we can apply to the provisions for existing businesses. It will be very difficult to assess to what extent any improvement in Grand Met's operating performance over the next few years is a fundamental improvement caused by efficiency gains which arise from the reorganisation, or whether the utilisation of the provisions is simply giving a rather more direct, albeit temporary, boost to performance by covering costs.

The ASB published a discussion paper on provisions in November 1995 which may restrict companies' ability in future to abuse the use of provisioning for reorganisation of ongoing businesses. In particular, the paper proposes that before companies can raise a reorganisation provision they must be committed to the expenditure rather than just intending to spend it. For example, there must be a detailed plan in place for the reorganisation and the plan should be publicly announced or already under way. Provisions should not be raised for anticipated future trading losses.

Although this discussion paper should improve matters if it is implemented, it will still leave companies able to raise reorganisation provisions. Investors should not ignore these but rather apply a modified version of the quantity test suggested in Chapter 4 for acquisition adjustments, namely to discount future profits of the company by the amount of the provisions in rating the shares until the provisions are exhausted.

STATEMENT OF RECOGNISED GAINS AND LOSSES

One major advantage to users of accounts provided by FRS 3 was the requirement for a statement of total recognised gains and losses. Since this statement included all movements in reserves, it brought into a single statement the items which many techniques of creative accounting frequently hid amongst the reserve movements in the balance sheet. It is one of the common features of creative techniques that they attempt not only to remove losses from 'above the line' at which EPS are calculated, but also to take them out of the profit & loss account altogether and place them in the balance sheet. Good examples are transferring loss-making assets from current to fixed assets (Chapter 13) and currency mismatching or interest rate arbitrage (Chapter 14).

In the first edition of *Accounting for Growth* there was an early guesstimate of the impact which the new statement of total recognised gains and losses

Exhibit 7.3 **Fisons 1990**	
	1990
	£m
Attributable Profit	169.0
Goodwill written off to Reserves	(284.4)
Intangible assets written off	(118.9)
Amounts realised on properties	(0.3)
Exchange losses	(8.1)
Total recognised gains and losses	(142.7)
Dividends	(51.5)
Net decrease in shareholders' funds	(194.2)
Total recognised loss per share	(21.0p)

would make using Fisons as an example (See Exhibit 7.3).

Fisons reported EPS of 26.3p for 1990, whereas the total loss per share shown by the estimated statement of total recognised gains and losses was

21p. The inclusion of the dividend in the statement made this comparison less than exact, and the goodwill on Fisons' acquisition of VG Instruments and intangibles written off were probably one-offs rather than genuine revenue items. But even so, the statement enables the reader to see some debit items which would have only appeared in the reserves notes to the balance sheet previously, such as the loss realised on properties and exchange losses. As such it warrants rather more attention by investors who want to spot companies' attempts to bolster the profit & loss account at the expense of the balance sheet than I suspect it receives.

IIMR AND OTHER EARNINGS MEASURES

Part of the ASB's intention in changing the structure of the profit & loss account with FRS 3 was perhaps to bring home to readers of accounts some fundamental truths about companies' performance. It was hoped that readers of accounts would be shifted away from the single number of EPS as a measure of company performance. Despite its position as a holy grail for the assessment of company performance and value through the PE multiple, earnings per share growth has many limitations. For example, it only measures growth without any consideration of the return achieved on the capital which is involved in delivering that growth, which can only be measured through return calculations such as return on capital or return on equity.

The ASB may have hoped that once presented with several possible earnings figures for a company (companies are able to present their own version of EPS alongside the FRS 3 number providing the calculation of their own number is consistent over time and reconciled with the FRS 3 number, and several other versions have also arisen) and an FRS 3 earnings figure which lumped together what would have been both extraordinary and exceptional items 'above the line' and included them in the calculation of EPS, investors would be more likely to appreciate that it is difficult to assess a company's performance from a single number.

Certainly, the propensity of FRS 3 earnings to gyrate more wildly due to the inclusion of what would have been (legitimately or otherwise) extraordinary items in the earnings figure has underlined the fact that company profits do often have an erratic course, and do not exhibit the smooth upward progression which was often achieved using the licence provided by SSAP 6 to shove inconvenient negative items below the line.

The trouble is that human beings crave simplicity, and rarely more so than in financial matters. Consequently, the explosion of the profit & loss account into potentially numerous different profits and earnings measures was accompanied by a move by the Institute of Investment Management and Research (the IIMR, the analysts' professional body) and many large broking houses to devise a new single figure measure of earnings performance. What is being sought is some form of 'sustainable', 'maintainable' or 'normalised' earnings. Thus, the IIMR Headline earnings figures exclude costs of fundamental reorganisations, discontinued businesses and profits or losses on the sale of fixed assets or businesses in an effort to get some measure of regular trading earnings. This certainly serves a purpose. Without a single, objective measure of earnings it would be impossible to calculate the PE of a sector or the market to compare an individual company with in terms of relative valuation.

But there is a risk that any formulaic approach to obtaining a single earnings figure which does not gyrate too wildly will deflect investors and other users of accounts from using the post FRS 3 profit & loss account as they should to look at the company's earnings performance from several directions, and attempt to value the company in the light of the fluctuations in its reported profits rather than in spite of them.

8

CASH FLOW ACCOUNTING

We get suspicious when a business reports profits without generating cash.
Lord Weinstock

In the chapter on Survival Techniques in the Accounting Jungle in the first edition of *Accounting for Growth* the phrase "Cash is king!" was embraced as one which could help the would-be investor in analysing company accounts. Many of the techniques of creative accountancy have the effect of generating reported profits without producing as much or any cash, so the investor should always test a company's solvency and valuation by some form of cash flow analysis.

Take for example the practice of raising acquisition or other provisions to cover 'reorganisation' costs. As these provisions are utilised to cover future costs, they will boost profits. But to the extent that the costs being incurred are cash costs such as redundancy payments, rather than just write-downs of asset values, removing these costs from the profit & loss account will mean that profits may provide a misleadingly optimistic picture of the cash the business is generating.

A less suspicious reason why profits often diverge from cash generated is the problem of working capital. When a company expands its sales the effect is not often to generate cash immediately, since it first needs to purchase stocks with which to attract buyers, and then needs to fund the buyers for a period of credit when they become debtors.

There are exceptions, such as much of the retail sector which has cash customers, but by and large, companies experience working capital strain as they grow.

Companies also need to invest in new fixed assets, and capital expenditure can be a drain on cash. A lot of rubbish is talked about looking at cash flow before capital expenditure since some or all capital expenditure is discretionary, so the cash flow before it is a measure of the cash generated which the business has at its disposal. In my view this is often mistaken. Since the calculation of cash flow involves adding depreciation (which is a non cash charge) to profits, it is asymmetrical not to deduct capital expenditure which is the cash flow equivalent of depreciation. Although some capital expenditure will often be of an expansionary nature, and therefore not truly equivalent to depreciation which measures the cost of maintaining assets, and some is discretionary, in my view very little capital expenditure is truly discretionary if a company wishes to maintain the competitiveness of its business.

So overall, I am a fan of cash flow analysis. It would therefore be churlish of me not to welcome the ASB's first Financial Reporting Standard, FRS 1, which introduced the cash flow statement to company accounts. FRS 1 had just arrived on the scene as the first edition went to press, and one of the earliest examples of a cash flow statement from Bass was analysed in the 'Survival Techniques' chapter.

BUT WHAT IS CASH?

It is one thing to accept that FRS 1 and cash flow statements have improved our ability to analyse companies, but a quite different proposition to believe that we can simply take the output of the cash flow statement at face value.

An example of a FT-SE 100 company which produced one of the earliest cash flow statements under FRS 1 illustrates this point. (See Exhibit 8.1)

The cash flow statement produced by Hanson for 1991 illustrates in rather extreme fashion the potential dangers in the FRS 1 cash flow statement. The following tables show extracts from various points in the Hanson cash flow. Which level of the cash flow statement should the reader take as representing the company's cash flow? Following the David Tweedie advice (see Chapter 2) and looking at the bottom line for Hanson in 1991 would produce a rather surprising result (See Exhibit 8.2).

Hanson shows a net cash inflow of £5.17bn in 1991 which seems rather large, particularly when it is compared with a few other figures in the accounts. Further up the cash flow statement, the net cash inflow in respect of operating activities (the nearest equivalent in the statement to the cash flow equivalent of operating profits) is shown as £934m (See Exhibit 8.3).

This seems a respectable cash flow, particularly since Hanson had trading profits of £937m in 1991. But it is a long way from the 'bottom line' cash flow of over £5bn. This figure looks all the more curious given that Hanson only had turnover of £7bn in 1991. The clue to this apparently massive cash inflow is to be found mid-way down the Statement (See Exhibit 8.4).

The clue is in the massive £6bn cash inflow from short-term investments. This brings home a problem in defining cash. Although cash is more

Exhibit 8.1 **Hanson Cash Flow Statement 1991**	
	Sep 30 1991
	£m
Operating Activities	934
Investment return and servicing of finance	
Assoc cos divs recd.	11
Interest received	929
Interest paid	(751)
Dividends paid	(507)
	(318)
Taxation	(255)
Investing activities	
Inflow in respect of short term investments	5932
Outflow in respect of short term investments	(2896)
Subsidiaries acquired	(704)
Investments acquired	(257)
Tangible assets acquired	(266)
Subsidiaries sold	90
Associated companies sold	-
Investments sold	843
Tangible assets sold	67
Misc investing inflow	-
	2,809
Net cash flow before financing	3,170
Financing	
Short Term debt raised	1,566
Long term debt raised	858
Share capital issued	13
Short Term loans repaid	(425)
Issue expenses	(12)
	2,000
Cash increase (decrease)	5,170
Currency appreciation	(95)
Balance Sheet Cash increase (decrease)	5,075

Exhibit 8.2 **Hanson Cash Flow Statement 1991**		
	1991	1990
	£m	£m
Cash increase (decrease) after financing	5,170	(1,601)

Exhibit 8.3 **Hanson Cash Flow Statement 1991**		
	1991	1990
	£m	£m
Net cash inflow from operating activities	934	712

Exhibit 8.4 **Hanson Cash Flow Statement 1991**		
	1991	1990
	£m	£m
Inflow in respect of short-term investments	5,932	3,334

difficult to manipulate than profits, even cash is not a simple concept. Is cash just notes and coin? Most individuals would not regard such a limited definition of cash as satisfactory, since they hold funds which are readily available in their bank accounts, and may have other sources of funds which could be tapped quickly if required, such as deposit accounts, bonds and shares. Companies are the same. Comparatively small amounts of funds will actually be held by companies literally in cash. The remainder will be in bank accounts or short-term investments where they can earn interest for the company whilst it is waiting to use them.

FRS 1 talks about cash and 'cash equivalents', meaning that it includes as cash a number of these short-term investments. The cut-off point taken for the maturity of a short-term investment is necessarily arbitrary. FRS 1 took three months, i.e. if an investment was within three months of maturing, such as a bank deposit for two months or Treasury bills with less than 90 days to repayment, they are treated as cash by FRS 1.

The natural consequence of this is that as an investment moves from over three months to maturity to under three months, for example, it generates a cash inflow. This is exactly what happened with Hanson. Hanson carried significant cash balances which were invested. As these investments moved to under three months maturity in 1991, they generated a cash inflow in terms of FRS 1. Of course, this was not a cash inflow in any sense that people would normally understand. If money you had on six months deposit moved as a result of the passage of time to under three months, would you regard yourself as having received a cash inflow? Probably not. What would have happened is that your cash resources would have moved closer to being freely disposable, not that they had actually grown in size. What FRS 1 does is to confuse two issues: the size of cash resources, and their availability.

To be fair, this problem with FRS 1 was spotted early in its life, but the

ASB resolved not to change it too soon, but rather to let the Standard run for a period to see whether other changes were necessary once more examples of its implementation were available. The results were published as Financial Reporting Exposure Draft (FRED) 10 in December 1995. Amongst the changes proposed by FRED 10 is a move to defining cash more simply as cash in hand plus deposits available on demand, such as current account balances.

Another innovation proposed by FRED 10 is a simpler layout for the cash flow statement which makes it easier to see the free cash flow, since there will be a sub-total within the statement after payment of interest, dividends and capital expenditure.

It may seem that the size of the discrepancy between Hansons's operating cash flow and the bottom line cash inflow after financing was so great that no one could have misunderstood. Maybe, but the Hanson example illustrates the point that even though I recommend cash flow analysis, and FRS 1 and now FRED 10 have made a great contribution to our ability to perform this analysis, there is no such thing as a perfect accounting standard, and you must remain alert and perform your own common-sense tests. The next company you encounter may not be showing such a large cash inflow from investments as to make it obvious, so you need to read the cash flow carefully even when the FRED 10 format is introduced, since who knows what wrinkles companies will find to use in the new standard? Common-sense tests include simple comparisons. For example, does the company's free cash flow appear realistic in relation to profits, or even sales?

The intriguing question with Hanson remains what was the actual cash flow in 1991? Whilst appreciating that comparing the stock of cash or debt on the balance sheet at the beginning and end of the year is not the same as measuring cash flow, the position revealed by performing this calculation for Hanson in 1991 is still intriguing:

Exhibit 8.5 **Hanson Change in Net Cash Position in 1990-91**		
	1990E	*1991E*
	£m	*£m*
Change in net (debt)/cash	1408	-209

The table shows that during 1991, Hanson's net debt/cash position changed by a £209m rise in net debt/fall in the cash position. Objectively, this is not really all that bad for an industrial conglomerate in the midst of a ferocious recession. But it is far cry from the operating cash inflow of £934m shown in the cash flow statement, or the £5bn net cash inflow after financing. This is precisely the sort of simple cross-check which can be performed to determine whether the cash flow statement is giving an accurate or even comprehensible picture.

This is another area where FRED 10 will provide more assistance since it will require companies to show the reconciliation between cash flow and changes in the balance sheet net debt position.

Until this is available, you should not be put off if you perform some calculations such as those shown above for Hanson's 'cash flow' and change in net debt and are then unable to reconcile the differences revealed. Always remember your final safeguard is that you do not have to invest. If you cannot satisfy yourself that the company is producing a cash flow concomitant with its profits, don't invest. If you read the cash flow statement and do not understand some of the figures ask the company, if you have the opportunity, by writing to them if necessary, or ask your broker to explain them. If you don't understand or like the response, don't invest. If you perform the calculation for change in net cash/debt that is shown above for Hanson and it reveals a similar contrast with the cash flow statement, ask for an explanation. And if you don't get one you understand and like. . . well you know the rest.

Figure 8.1   **Hanson share price relative to All Share Index**

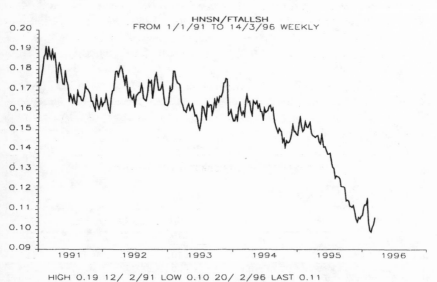

What is clear from subsequent events, including the proposed demerger of Hanson, is that it was not producing cash at anything like the rate that could be inferred from its inaugural Cash Flow Statement in 1991.

9

CONTINGENT LIABILITIES

Contingency: accident, casualty, chance, event, fortuity, happening, incident, possibility, uncertainty
Oxford English Dictionary

It is no coincidence that the term contingency has several meanings, most of which are close to common parlance for an accident. Most investors' grasp of contingent liabilities in the last few years has been accidental, and the outcome has often been disastrous.

A contingency is defined by SSAP18 as 'a condition which exists at the balance sheet date where the outcome will be confirmed only on the occurrence or non-occurrence of one or more uncertain future events'! Contingencies are not intended to cover the normal uncertainties associated with accounting estimates, such as a valuation of assets, the lives of assets, the amount of bad debts, etc. A contingency also requires uncertainty as to the outcome of an event, for example, where a company has litigation pending against it.

Frequently the last or penultimate Note in a set of Accounts, the Contingent Liabilities note often makes apparently dull reading. Certain types of contingency are disclosed almost in a litany, as a matter of course by most companies, for example:

Exhibit 9.1 **Lloyds Bank PLC 1990 Accounts**

27. Contingent Liabilities

	Group		Bank	
	1990	1989	1990	1989
	£m	£m	£m	£m
Acceptances	910	1,085	589	521
Guarantees and similar obligations	4,026	4,902	4,152	6,079
	4,936	5,987	4,741	6,600

In addition, contingent liabilities exist in respect of forward contracts for the sale and purchase of foreign currencies, financial futures, option contracts and other facilities to customers which are not reflected in the balance sheets.

Banks take on substantial contingent liabilities in their normal course of business, such as the issue of guarantees and indemnities and dealing with customers in financial instruments which only become exercisable in the future, such as forward foreign exchange markets, options, futures, etc. so that they nearly all have a common wording for these activities in the Contingent Liabilities note, but with little qualification:

COMMON TYPES OF CONTINGENT LIABILITIES

(a) Guarantees of subsidiary overdrafts: where a bank lends to a subsidiary within a group it will normally require the holding company's guarantee; otherwise if the subsidiary gets into difficulties the holding company could rely upon its limited liability as an equity holder in the subsidiary and walk away, leaving the bank with the loss.

(b) Performance bonds – many types of performance bond are required. For example a housebuilder will be required to supply a bond from its bank to ensure that the roads, drains etc. on an estate he constructs will be up to the standard that the local authority is willing to maintain subsequently. Since the bank will only issue such a bond if the builder counter-indemnifies it the builder will have a contingent liability to its bank if the bond is ever called.

(c) Discounted bills – where a company raises finance by selling (discounting) bills of exchange it has received or factoring debtors with recourse, the bank or finance house will have recourse to it if the bills or debts are not met at maturity. Having been on-sold, the bills do not appear on the company's balance sheet, but there should be a contingent liability shown.

Perhaps a typical example is contractor and developer Mowlem. (See Exhibit 9.2.) This shows the normal contingent liabilities that you might expect for a building contractor – bonds, loan guarantees and capital expenditure authorised. And the Note points out that Mowlem counter-indemnifies banks for bonds issued on its behalf.

Exhibit 9.2 **Mowlem 1990 Report and Accounts**

23. Guarantees and other financial commitments

	Group 1990 £m	Group 1989 £m	Company 1990 £m	Company 1989 £m
Loan guarantees outstanding in respect of subsidiary companies	-	-	60.5	65.2
Associated companies				
Bonding support	0.4	8.3	0.4	8.3
Loan Guarantees	26.7	7.6	26.7	6.9
	27.1	15.9	27.1	15.2
Capital Expenditure				
Contracted for	-	2.1	-	0.2
Authorised but not contracted for	4.7	2.5	-	1.4
	4.7	4.6	-	1.6

Annual commitment under non-cancellable operating leases are as follows:

	Group Land and buildings 1990 £m	Group Plant and machinery 1990 £m	Company Land and buildings 1989 £m	Company Plant and machinery 1989 £m	Land and buildings 1990 £m	Land and buildings 1990 £m
Operating leases which expire						
Within 1 year	0.6	2.6	0.3	2.1	-	-
In 2 to 5 years	2.0	10.3	0.8	10.2	-	-
Over 5 years	3.4	5.8	4.4	0.5	1.1	1.1
	6.0	18.7	5.5	12.8	1.1	1.1

The Company issued counter-indemnities to financial institutions in respect of tender, advance payment, retention and performance bonds. Terms and conditions of such bonds vary but may prescribe payment on demand. Contractual commitments have been entered into by the Company which, by agreement, have been performed by and reflected in the accounts of its subsidiaries.

But as in the accounts for another builder and developer, Costain Group, a much more dangerous item may lurk behind the contingent liabilities Note:

Exhibit 9.3   **Costain Group 1990 Report & Accounts**

27. Contingent Liabilities

	Group		Company	
	1990	1989	1990	1989
	£m	£m	£m	£m
Under guarantee of bank overdrafts, mortgages and loans:				
To subsidiary undertakings	-	-	98.2	122.8
To associated undertakings	52.0	28.2	52.0	28.2
To long-term joint ventures	-	1.5	-	1.5
To other joint ventures	19.1	4.6	19.1	4.6

There are also contingent liabilities in respect of:

The creditors of joint ventures which are less than the book value of their assets.

Performance bonds and other undertakings entered into in the ordinary course of business.

Preference shares issued by a subsidiary undertaking (note 24).

No security has been given in respect of any guarantee given by the Group.

The Note mentions liabilities for guarantees to banks of borrowings by associates, and other contingent liabilities for joint ventures in the form of bank guarantees and creditors. But Costain is a member of the Trans-Manche Link (TML) consortium which constructed the Channel Tunnel. TML has been in dispute with Eurotunnel in respect of claims for over £1bn, the outcome of which could clearly affect the solvency of a company such as Costain and other members of TML, such as Tarmac, Taylor Woodrow, Wimpey and Balfour Beatty (part of BICC). This is hardly discernible from Costain's apparently anodyne contingent liabilities note.

And as with other accounting practices, failing to pay due regard to contingent liabilities can prove fatal or just expensive:

The example of Coloroll was cited in the section on the Pre-Acquisition Write Down in the first edition. A fuller history of Coloroll's rise and fall is given in Appendix I. This reveals that in an attempt to reduce debt after its acquisition splurge, Coloroll 'sold' the cloth and clothing divisions of the recently acquired John Crowther Group. The sale was to an MBO called Response Group Limited, and as a consideration, Coloroll received £53m cash, £7.5m of redeemable preference shares in Response and £14.25m of loan notes issued by Response, plus £1m of shares in Response. At this point, Coloroll had not so much sold the Crowther interests to Response, as exchanged the Crowther interests for a share in Response. Consequently, Coloroll, on-sold the loan notes and redeemable preference shares 'with recourse' i.e. the purchaser could ask for their money back from Coloroll, which they duly did when the Response MBO hit financial problems in January 1990:

Exhibit 9.4   **Coloroll 1989 Report and Accounts**

23. Contingent liabilities

At 31 March 1989 the group had contingent liabilities in connection with the following matters:

(a) the sale with recourse of £7,500,000 of redeemable preference shares and £14,250,000 senior and subordinated loan notes in Response Group Limited which were received as part consideration for the sale of the clothing interests of John Crowther Group plc;

(b) the guarantee of borrowings and other bank facilities of Homfray Carpets Australia Pty Limited equivalent to £13,000,000 following the sale of the group's majority interest in that company. The guarantee provides for recourse by the group to the assets of Homfray Carpets Australia Pty Limited by way of a second charge;

(c) the guarantee of borrowings of £4,580,000 of the purchaser of land for development from the group (see note 6);

(d) the guarantee of borrowings of the owners of properties occupied by a subsidiary which at 31 March 1989 amounted to £1,150,000 (1988 £1,141,000).

By this time the liability had become £22m as the loan notes yielded 12 per cent payable as a premium upon redemption. The disclosure of this item in Coloroll's Note on contingent liabilities reveals that similar liabilities had been assumed in order to sell other assets; the guarantee of Homfray Carpets' bank borrowings in order to sell a *minority* interest in the company and a guarantee of borrowings for the purchaser of land sold by the group.

The question has to be asked whether an ordinary individual would consider that he had sold his house if he guaranteed repayment of the mortgage of the purchaser. Clearly he would not be free of the liabilities which went with the asset. If Coloroll was only able to sell assets such as Response MBO's preference shares by guaranteeing to repurchase them in the event of a default by Response, it is equally evident that there was something deeply wrong with the Response Group if a 'clean' sale could not be achieved.

So contingent liabilities need to be carefully examined. But unfortunately even that is not always a guarantee of protection for investors:

Exhibit 9.5   Allied Lyons Report and Accounts 1990

29. CONTINGENT LIABILITIES

	1990 £m	1989 £m
Group		
Guarantees by the company and by subsidiary companies, uncalled liability in respect of partly paid shares and bills discounted by group companies	79	67
Parent company		
Guarantees of stocks, bonds and notes of subsidiary companies	163	144
Value added tax of certain subsidiary companies under group registration scheme	28	22

No security has been given in respect of any contingent liability

---

The Contingent Liabilities Note for Allied Lyons seems reasonably revealing. It even shows that Allied Lyons is part of a VAT group with certain group subsidiary companies, and therefore has joint and several liability for the payment of the group VAT. What it does not reveal is the foreign currency transactions undertaken by the group treasury which cost the group £147m and led to the resignation of the Finance Director and early retirement by the Chairman.

Why was this massive foreign exchange transaction not revealed by the Contingent Liabilities Note? Because contingent liabilities by definition do not form part of the double-entry bookkeeping system which is at the heart of all accounting. Normal transactions are recorded by posting (or writing in a ledger or in this automated age typing into a computer record) equal and opposite entries – 'for every debit there is a credit' should be engraved above the bed of every junior accountant. So that when, for example, a company purchases a property using funds borrowed from a bank, the assets are increased by the cost of the property, and liabilities are increased by the amount of the bank borrowing.

Contingent liabilities by definition are liabilities which *may* become concrete in the future. Consequently, there are no equal and opposite assets, and no entry in the double-entry bookkeeping system which can be checked by the mechanism of a trial balance which auditors use: adding up all the debit items and all the credit items to see if they balance. This should reveal any unrecorded liabilities for a transaction which has taken place, since debit and credits would then fail to balance. Because of this absence of a need for double-entry bookkeeping for contingent liabilities, even major public companies may have their contingent liabilities recorded in a simple card index system, and the auditors are reliant upon the Directors' assurances that all contingent liabilities have been recorded and revealed.

The great grand-daddy of recent disasters substantially caused by unrecorded contingent liabilities was probably the collapse of British and Commonwealth:

Exhibit 9.6   British & Commonwealth Report & Accounts 1988

26. CONTINGENT LIABILITIES

a) The company has guaranteed bank overdrafts and other substantial trading liabilities of certain subsidiaries which have arisen in the normal course of their business and which are not expected to give any financial loss.

b) The directors are confident that there is no contingent liability arising out of counterclaims by Quadrex Holdings in respect of proceedings referred to in note 11.

Few Contingent Liability Notes could appear more innocuous than B&C's in 1988, with the usual litany about guaranteeing bank overdrafts and trading liabilities of certain subsidiaries. The only specific item mentioned was legal action against Quadrex which had failed to complete a deal to buy the money broking interest of B&C's Mercantile House acquisition. No numbers were mentioned at all.

But during July 1988, B&C had taken over Atlantic Computers plc. Atlantic started life in 1975 as a computer consultancy, founded by John Foulston, moving into computer leasing and eventually controlling an estimated 70 per cent of the UK computer leasing market. Foulston remained the entrepreneurial drive behind the company until his death in a motor racing accident at the Brands Hatch circuit, which he owned, in September 1987. The company was taken over by B&C the following year.

The cornerstone of Atlantic's business was the 'Flexlease' contract. Atlantic acted as an intermediary between the banks who were willing to lease computer equipment (just another form of lending, similar to hire purchase, as far as the bank is concerned) and the lessee who uses the equipment.

Atlantic's Flexlease was a separate contract with the lessee/user. The original lease might typically be for a period of seven years. Flexlease gave the user two additional options: 1) the 'Flex' – this allowed the user to return the equipment after three years providing he leased replacement equipment of greater value, and 2) the 'Walk' which enabled the user simply to terminate the lease by handing the equipment back to Atlantic after five years, leaving Atlantic to service the original lease payments to the bank.

Atlantic could cover its liability after the 'Walk' option was exercised to meet the payments to the bank under the original lease, firstly from sale of the equipment, although the residual or second-hand value of the equipment was rarely sufficient to meet this liability. If the user was exercising the Flex option, Atlantic would of course also have the income on the lease of the new equipment although this was not available if the user had 'Walked'. Thus Atlantic's operations became virtually a form of pyramid selling with the liabilities on original leases which Atlantic had to cover because a Flex option had been exercised, covered by payments under a new lease.

As an aside, there was often customer resistance to the higher lease payment required on the new lease under the Flex option. Atlantic usually overcame this by setting lease payments in the initial years of the new lease at the same level as the old lease, with a rapid escalation in the later years of the lease. But these higher payments in later years were often never reached as the user Flexed again or Walked so that the higher payments were never received. No wonder Atlantic's Flexlease gave it such a high market share! It gave users the flexibility which they they wanted during a period when upgrading of computer systems was rife due to technological change.

But the outcome for Atlantic was a burgeoning set of contingent liabilities to meet the payments due to banks on leases on which the lessees might Walk or Flex, which could only be covered by leasing ever greater amounts of new equipment.

But there was no sign of this contingent liability in the accounts of Atlantic or B&C. This apparent omission also called into question the diligence exercised when B&C acquired Atlantic in an agreed takeover i.e. one in which B&C had full access to Atlantic's books.

The dénouement rapidly followed. Immediately after Easter 1990, B&C announced that Atlantic was to go into administration less than one year after it was acquired. At the same time B&C wrote off some $550m to cover the cost of the original investment plus capital subsequently injected. It had, it claimed, 'ring-fenced' Atlantic to save the group – a polite way of saying that it was relying upon the principle of limited liability as an equity investor in its subsidiary and walking away to let the banks pick up the pieces.

But it was not as easy to erect a so-called 'ring-fence', as the advisers to Mirror Group have also now found as a result of the Maxwell débâcle. As can be seen in the table in Appendix II, B&C was a heavily indebted company and the liquidation of a subsidiary of the size of Atlantic produced fears that the trustees of B&C's bonds would be forced to call an event of default (company borrowings by means of bond issues are governed by trust deeds which define events of default such as the failure to pay interest on the bonds, and less obvious events such as the liquidation of major subsidiaries, sale of assets, etc. which could endanger the bond holders' interests and also require repayment), as well as unrest among B&C's bankers. The final nail in the coffin came on 1 June when the Securities and Investment Board (SIB) removed British & Commonwealth Merchant Bank (BCMB) from the list of banks authorised to accept clients' money under the Financial Services Act. This threatened a classic liquidity crisis for BCMB, and the response to this and the withdrawal of a £70m standby facility for BCMB from three major banks, triggered B&C's administration on 3 June.

Not bad going for a liability which was not shown in the accounts.

Contingent liabilities remain a common factor in the accounts of companies which fail or are in distress. Queens Moat Houses found itself in such dire condition in 1992 that the share price fell precipitously and was suspended and the group was only able to trade with the help of its bankers.

Exhibit 9.7 **Queens Moat Houses Report and Accounts 1992**

"Contingent liabilities have been rigorously reviewed in order to ascertain whether they are in fact actual liabilities, for which provision should be made in the accounts. In the light of the group's financial position, your board has reviewed and continues to review its actual and contingent liabilities very carefully."

An example of contingent liabilities which needed to be treated as actual in the 1992 annual report were exposures to interest rate and foreign exchange contracts which cost £16.7m to terminate.

In reviewing this chapter on contingent liabilities I am reminded of an old joke about a man who was lost in a hot air balloon. Fortunately he saw someone walking in a field below him so he lost height and when he was within range shouted "Can you tell me where I am?". The walker stopped, paused for thought, and shouted back "You're up in a hot air balloon." "You must be an accountant" retorted the balloonist. "Amazing", said the walker. "How did you know that?" "Because the information you just gave me was both totally accurate and completely useless!"

The joke can of course be adapted to the profession which you wish to make the butt of your wit, but the point of it for me is that even if the reader now grasps that contingent liabilities can be very dangerous for his wealth, how can he seek to avoid companies which have them, given the evident paucity of reporting this item in accounts?

Fairly obviously, reading the contingent liabilities note is important. In some cases, such as Coloroll, the dangers involved are all too clearly spelled out: it's just that investors rarely take the time or make the effort to read the accounts thoroughly. Moreover, if you do come across a Contingent Liabilities Note such that in the Coloroll accounts for the sale of the Response Group and Homfray Carpets you should be concerned not only by the size of the potential liabilities, but also that the company is in a position where it has to do deals which are not clean cut and leave it with such liabilities. It is often a sign that a company is in difficulties.

But what protection is there for an investor when a company is engaging in activities which bring liabilities such as B&C did with Atlantic Computers, or Barings with Nick Leeson's derivative trades, which are not mentioned specifically or quantified in the contingent liabilities note? Think about what the note will say in those circumstances. The company will probably fail to disclose these major liabilities by hiding behind the fig-leaf of the litany about engaging in certain types of activity in the normal course of business, e.g. guarantees, bonds, foreign exchange contracts, futures, etc. Which begs the question: how much do you understand about the company's 'normal activities'? If the company has recently bought a computer leasing subsidiary, do you understand how that business works, and the risks involved? Similarly, with regard to building contractors: you might understand the risks involved when the company has given a bond to guarantee that it will fulfil its obligations to put in roads and sewers on a new housing estate. But what if it is building the Channel Tunnel?

What this is heading towards is something close to an old and in my view good axiom of investment, which is not to invest in anything you don't understand. You are most unlikely to have understood how Barings made money. You should have known it was engaged in 'normal' merchant banking activities such as corporate finance and fund management. But without doubt the greatest growth area for its profits in the past decade was Baring Securities. What did they do? You were most unlikely to have understood what they did, something you would apparently have had in common with most of the City.

10

CAPITALISATION OF COSTS

or How to make an expense become an asset

Many different expenditures may be capitalised, although by far the commonest capitalised cost is interest on property under development. Capitalisation is a process by which an item would otherwise be seen as an expense or debit in the profit and loss account is instead classified as an asset in the balance sheet. As with all the accounting treatments described, capitalisation of costs is a legitimate technique. The Companies Act 1985 allows the inclusion in the cost of production of an asset of:

(a) a reasonable proportion of the costs incurred by the company which are only indirectly attributable to the production of that asset; and

(b) interest on capital borrowed to finance the production of that asset, to the extent that it accrues in respect of the period of production.

The Listing Agreement requires disclosure of interest capitalised by companies listed on the International Stock Exchange.

Exhibit 10.1 **Guinness 1989 Report & Accounts**

16. STOCKS

	1989 £m	1988 £m
Raw materials and consumables	134	105
Work in progress	28	19
Stocks of maturing whisky	1,085	860
Finished goods and goods for resale	169	144
	1,416	1,128

Stocks of maturing whisky include financing costs amounting to £481 m (1988 £417m). A net adjustment to stocks of £10m (1988 £12m) has been credited to the profit and loss account comprising £97m (1988 £98m) of interest incurred during the year less £87m (1988 £86m) in respect of sales during the year. Following the review of the Distillers fair value accounting (Note 11) the amount at which maturing whisky stocks are stated as at 31 December 1989 has been uplifted by £157m including £49m relating to financing costs.

CAPITALISING INTEREST

This is a practice normally associated with property development or the construction of properties for the use in a business e.g. stores or supermarkets but there are other uses. For example, ships, aircraft and stocks of goods which take a long time to mature such as whisky.

But capitalisation of interest on property development was the commonest form of capitalisation of costs prior to the recession:

Table 10.1   Quoted Property Companies

Company	Year to	Net Interest Total	Capitalised	Pre-tax Profit
British Land	Mar 91	61.4	1.3	31.0
Great Portland	Mar 91	16.1	nil	33.8
Hammerson	Dec 90	70.8	29.8	70.7
Land Securities	Mar 91	79.1	nil	215.2
MEPC	Sep 91	119.2	39.5	143.3
Slough	Dec 90	84.3	59.8	22.6

Capitalisation of interest remained common practice within the sector, although it was never adopted by the largest company Land Securities. The practice was also dropped by Great Portland and by smaller companies such as Property Security Investment Trust. Their reasons are worth considering:

Exhibit 10.2   **Statement by the Chairman – Property Security Investment Trust**

A conservative accounting policy has always been the byword for the Company. Interest and other costs on investment properties being developed are written off against Revenue. On the other hand interest in developing dealing properties was capitalised. *That was justifiable in a buoyant market,* but the economic climate has now changed. To extend the conservative approach your Board has decided to change the Company's accounting policy so that from the commencement of the current financial year interest on all dealing properties will no longer be capitalised but charged against revenue.

The obvious problem which these companies can encounter is that the cost of the property plus capitalised interest can easily exceed the market value, which leads to write-downs of the difference by which cost exceeds market.

The argument for capitalisation is that interest is a legitimate cost of the project and therefore it is as appropriate to capitalise as the cost of bricks and mortar. Witness the fact that no property developer ever computes the viability of a project without including the cost of interest until the project is complete and/or sold.

Where property is under construction for use in a company's activities, such as a hotel or store, it is also argued that capitalising interest gives a better match between income and expense in future since the interest cost only begins to bear on the profit and loss account once the project is complete and generating income.

Exhibit 10.3 **Broadwell Land 1989 Accounts**

CONSOLIDATED PROFIT & LOSS ACCOUNT 1989
for the year to 31 March, 1989

	Notes	1989 £	1988 £
Turnover	1	33,678,720	16,864,484
Operating expenses	2	(26,719,406)	(12,703,965)
Operating profit		6,959,314	4,160,519
Interest receivable	4	244,459	24,222
Interest payable	5	(148,270)	(39,585)
Profit on ordinary activities before taxation		7,055,503	4,145,156
Taxation	6	(2,510,406)	(1,447,097)
Profit for the year after taxation		4,545,097	2,698,059
Dividends	7	(1,280,582)	(65,700)
Retained profit for the year	21	3,264,515	2,632,359
Earnings per share – basic	8	19.08p	14.35p

The comparative figures for 1988 have been restated to comply with Statement of Standard Accounting Practice 9 (revised).

Broadwell Land 1989 Accounts

5. Interest payable

	1989 £	1988 £
On bank loans, overdrafts and other loans:		
Payable within five years	3,892,684	1,456,032
Less: Interest added to developments-in-progress	(2,215,024)	(979,520)
Interest included as a cost of sale of developments	(1,270,195)	(436,927)
Interest capitalised in investment properties	(152,886)	-
Interest capitalised in other tangible fixed assets	(107,309)	-
	148,270	39,585

Exhibit 10.4   **Rockfort Group 1989 Report & Accounts**

8. INTEREST PAYABLE AND SIMILAR CHARGES

	1989 £000	1988 £000
Interest on bank loans and overdrafts		
Repayable otherwise than by instalments within five years	2,455	748
Repayable by instalments wholly within five years	509	547
Other interest	240	152
Licence fee	1,637	222
	4,841	1,669
Less: interest capitalised on development land and properties	1,288	702
	3,553	967

Rush & Tompkins Group 1989 Report & Accounts

4. INTEREST

	1989 £000	1988 £000
On bank loans, overdrafts and finance leases:		
Repayable within 5 years, not by instalments	11,697	5,678
Repayable within 5 years by instalments	145	155
	11,842	5,833
Interest receivable	1,972	711
Net interest payable for the year	9,870	5,122
Less: interest added to developments in progress	8,521	3,885
Net interest charged in the profit and loss account	1,349	1,237
Share of related companies interest included above:		
Net interest payable	7,240	2,810
Less: interest added to developments in progress	5,737	2,037
Net interest charged in the profit and loss account	1,503	773

Finally, it is worth noting that if companies were not permitted to capitalise interest there would be a lower asset cost but also a lower profit (because interest would be charged through the profit and loss account) for a company which built its own factory or hotel, compared with the same company if it purchased the property once completed by a developer (who would certainly seek to include his interest cost in computing the sale price).

There are counter arguments, but these are much less important than simply understanding the impact of capitalised interest in published accounts, as illustrated in Exhibit 10.3 on the previus page.

Interest cover is an important measure of the financial health of a company. It measures the company's ability to cover the interest payments due to its bankers, and the margin of cover if profits should fall. Normally it is calculated by dividing operating profit by net interest payable. But Broadwell Land ostensibly had no problem confronting this measure in 1989: there was no net interest payable, with interest receivable of £244,459 and interest payable of £148,270 to give *net* interest receivable of £96,189 against operating profit of £6,959,314, as shown in the Profit and Loss Account.

But Note 5 reveals that the actual interest payable was £3,893,684, all but £148,270 of which was capitalised. Ignoring capitalised interest, i.e. bringing it back into the profit and loss account, gives a very different interest cover computation:

Interest payable of £3,893,684 minus interest receivable of £244,459 = net interest payable of £3,649,225

Operating profit £6,959,314/£3,649,225 = 1.9 times cover

This can hardly be considered generous. Interest cover below two times would usually be regarded as a warning signal. This is even more true when profits are at a speculative peak, which was demonstrated in 1990 when property profits collapsed and Broadwell Land went into administrative receivership.

An analysis of 45 listed, USM or Third Market companies which had receivers or administrative receivers appointed in 1989 and 1990 shows the following pattern for interest cover in the final year before they were declared insolvent.

Table 10.2   Interest cover

Cover	Number of Companies
No cover	6
Under 1x	1
1x – 2x	14
2x – 3x	6
3x – 4x	5
over 4x	13

Sixty per cent were less than three times covered in their final accounts.

There are plenty of examples of capitalised interest from property developers and others (See Exhibit 10.5) which was one of the factors which disguised the precarious nature of a company's finances. The following table

Exhibit 10.5   Citygrove 1989 Report & Accounts

3. INTEREST PAYABLE

	1989 £000	1988 £000
Loans repayable wholly or in part over five years	33	30
Bank overdraft and loans repayable wholly or in part within five years	4,829	1,877
Hire purchase and finance lease interest	82	45
Other interest	-	2
	4,944	1,954
Less: Interest capitalised	(1,448)	(258)
	3,496	1,696

Kentish Property Group 1987 Report & Accounts

3. INTEREST PAYABLE AND SIMILAR CHARGES

	1987 £000	1986 £000
On bank overdrafts and short-term borrowing	2,313	794
On directors' loans	-	14
Other loans	4	15
	2,347	823
Included as cost of sales and capitalised	(2,292)	(776)
	52	47

Leading Leisure 1989 Report & Accounts

4. NET INTEREST PAYABLE

	14 months 31 December 1989 £000	12 months 31 October 1988 £000
On bank loans and overdrafts repayable wholly within five years	4,347	525
On bank loans and overdrafts repayable partly after five years	6,995	3,462
On other loans	588	340
Interest capitalised	(6,412)	(1,903)
Interest receivable	(643)	(17)
	4,875	2,407

Reliant 1989 Report & Accounts

3. INTEREST PAYABLE

	Group 1989 £000	1988 £000
Bank loans and overdrafts wholly payable within five years	3,082	1,279
Other loans	37	57
Finance lease charges	31	16
	3,150	1,352
Capitalised	(2,494)	(978)
	656	374

shows the capitalised interest position and true interest cover ignoring capitalised interest, for companies which have all been placed in receivership or administrative receivership:

Table 10.3   True interest cover

Company	Capitalised interest as a percentage of operating profit %	Interest cover in profit or loss account x	Interest cover taking capitalised interest into paid x
Broadwell Land	53.8	-*	1.9
Citygrove	31.3	2.0	1.4
Kentish Properties	57.6	-*	1.7
Leading Leisure	53.5	2.5	1.1
Reliant	75.3	5.1	1.1
Rockfort	19.3	3.5	2.1
Rush & Tompkins	88.1	7.2	1.0

* net interest receivable in the profit and loss account.

In all cases the actual interest was obviously significantly lower once capitalised interest is taken into account, and dangerously low to withstand a downturn in profits.

Ignoring the use of capitalised interest, and the calculation of interest cover from the net interest payable shown in the profit and loss account can be dangerous. The bankers who lend the money and make the decision on whether companies survive during a downturn include capitalised interest in their calculations of cover. And if investors wish to understand how the decisions of the banks are likely to impact their investments it is necessary to understand their methods of analysis. The banker is not interested in whether his quarterly interest charge is capitalised as part of an asset or is expensed in the profit and loss account. His sole interest is in cash: is there enough cash coming in to cover the whole of the interest charged to the company's account? If not, there is a problem.

Obviously including (i.e. adding back) capitalised interest in the calculation of interest cover helps to get closer to the banker's viewpoint, although even then the assumption that operating profit is equal to cash inflow is far from realistic (see Chapter 8).

Capitalisation of interest is not confined to the property development sector. There are examples above of companies in other areas such as leisure and motor manufacturing. A list of capitalised interest as a proportion of pre-tax (operating) profit shows the following major companies were involved in this practice at the beginning of the recession:

Table 10.4 Capitalised interest

Company	Year	Capitalised interest as a percentage of pre-tax profits %
Stakis	1990	89.5
Costain	1990	87.3
ABP	1990	59.5
Ladbroke	1990	27.1
Enterprise Oil	1990	23.2
Asda	1990	21.1
Queens Moat House	1990	19.5
Burton	1990	19.0
BAA	1990	18.6
Lasmo	1990	13.6
Clyde Petroleum	1990	12.6
Wm Morrison Supermarket	1991	11.5
Forte	1991	10.7
Taylor Woodrow	1990	10.4
J Sainsbury	1991	10.1

The list is dominated by companies from a few industries: Hotels – Stakis, Ladbroke, Queens Moat Houses, Forte; Oil – Enterprise, Lasmo, Clyde; Food Retailing – Asda, Wm Morrison; and Construction – Costain and Taylor Woodrow. Obviously some of these industries are particularly identified with the development of premises for the company's use and most notably hotels and hyper-markets in food retailing which had particularly high development expenditure in 1991 from the capital raised by the main food retailing groups. Some of these companies have now stopped this practice.

Capitalisation of interest also produces problems of comparability between companies using the technique. It is possible to have wide variations between when a company may begin to capitalise interest on a project and to end it:

Start of capitalisation	*End of capitalisation*
Exchange of contracts on a development site	When the property is completed
Completion of a purchase of a site	When the property is fully let
When planning consent is obtained	When trading commences
Upon entering into a building contract	When the property is x% let
Commencement of work	When rental income equates to x% of that anticipated
	When rental income exceeds interest

Nor is interest only capitalised on property. Corton Beach took this concept a stage further as its Accounting Policy Notes indicate:

Exhibit 10.6 **Corton Beach 1990 Report & Accounts**

(b) Basis of consolidation

The Group financial statements consolidate the financial statements of the Company and all its subsidiaries made up to 31 January 1990.

The result of the subsidiaries acquired or disposed of are included in the Group profit and loss account from the date of acquisition or up to the date of disposal. At the acquisition date the fair values of the net assets, excluding goodwill, are determined and these values are incorporated in the Group financial statements. The excess of the purchase consideration (including costs of acquisition and due provision for reorganisation costs) over the fair value of assets acquired (after due provision is made for all potential liabilities, asset write down and asset revaluations) represent goodwill (for further explanations see 1(f) below).

Interest relating to acquisitions is capitalised, as part of the acquisition cost, from the effective date of acquisition until the acquired company is substantially integrated within the Group, or for one year, whichever is sooner. The amount of such capitalised interest for the year ending 31 January 1990 was £757,000 (1989 nil).

No profit and loss account is presented for the Company as provided by S229(7) of the Companies Act 1985. Of the Group profit for the financial year £1,021,000 (1989 £187,000) has been dealt with in the accounts of the Company.

This is a novel concept: that where a subsidiary is acquired for debt, the interest on the debt should be capitalised until the acquisition is fully integrated into the group (whatever that means). This seems to be taking to extremes the concept that capitalisation of interest is designed to protect the profit and loss account from distortion whilst an asset generates rent or trading income. Corton Beach presumably had some income from its acquisition prior to 'full integration'. Corton Beach is now in administrative receivership.

CAPITALISING OTHER COSTS

Interest is not the only cost which companies can capitalise. SSAP13 permits the capitalisation of research and development expenditure which may affect drug companies, electronics, biotechnology, engineering etc.

Exhibit 10.7 **Siebe Annual Report and Accounts 1994**

Research and development expenditure

Expenditure on research and development is written off when incurred except for development prototype expenditure and associated software costs on defined commercial projects.

Nonetheless not all companies with substantial R&D expenditure take advantage of the possibility of capitalising it:

Exhibit 10.8 **SmithKline Beecham Annual Report 1993**

Research and development expenditure

Laboratory buildings and equipment used for research and development are included as fixed assets and written off in accordance with the Group's depreciation policy. Other research and development expenditure is written off in the year in which it is incurred.

SmithKline Beecham showed research and development expenditure of £390m as an expense in the profit and loss account, capitalising only the laboratory buildings and equipment used for research work.

Contrast this with the treatment adopted by Rockwood, another company which has gone into administrative receivership. Rockwood was a holding company engaged in freight forwarding, distribution, warehousing and security – hardly high-tech companies. It, nonetheless, capitalised patents and development expenditure to the tune of £957,000 (see Exhibit 10.9).

What harm does it do? MTM the speciality chemicals group announced in March 1992 that its results for 1991 would be substantially below expectations, and that the announcement of these results would be delayed. The reason given was that the auditors wished to change certain accounting policies, particularly relating to MTM's capitalisation of product registration and development costs.

Exhibit 10.9 Rockwood 1988 Accounts

10. Intangibles

	Development cost £000	Other £000	Total £000
Group			
Cost at 1 January 1988	159	190	349
Additions	586	22	608
At 31 December 1988	745	212	957

Other intangible fixed assets consist of patents held by the Hilton Gun Company. The development expenditure is principally incurred by the Defence Systems group and relates to initial set-up costs in new areas of activity.

Note c) DEPRECIATION AND AMORTISATION

Depreciation is provided by equal annual instalments to write off the purchase costs over the expected useful life of assets. The useful life assumed for freehold buildings is 50 years for leasehold property over 50 years. For fixtures and fittings it is 10 years and for motor vehicles it is between 4 and 7 years. Freehold land is not depreciated.

Intangible assets comprise patents and development costs, which are written off to profit and loss accounts over the appropriate period between 3 and 10 years.

The immediate impact on MTM's share price from this announcement is obvious:

Figure 10.1   MTM share price chart 1992

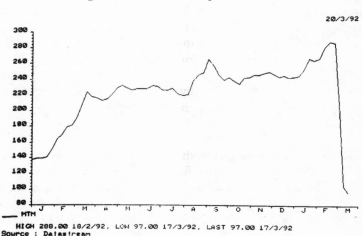

HIGH 289.00 18/2/92, LOW 97.00 17/3/92, LAST 97.00 17/3/92
Source : Datastream

Exhibit 10.10   **MTM Report and Accounts 1990**

Note c) Intangible assets

Intangible fixed assets comprise product registration costs and development expenditure incurred by the Group. Amortisation of product and process development costs commences with commercial production by reference to the lesser of life of the product or process, or ten years. Upon commencement of commercial production the costs are transferred to tangible fixed assets.

Note 13. Intangible fixed assets

	Product & Process Development £000	Market Development £000	Total £000
Group			
Cost			
1 January 1990	2,217	140	2,357
Exchange adjustment	(10)	-	(10)
Additions	1,252	-	1,252
Acquisition of subsidiaries	24	-	24
Transfer to tangible fixed assets	(362)	-	(362)
31 December 1990	3,121	140	3,261
Depreciation			
1 January 1990	428	36	464
Charge for year	185	14	199
31 December 1990	613	50	663
Net book amount			
31 December 1990	2,508	90	2,598
31 December 1989	1,789	104	1,893
Company			
Cost			
1 January 1990 and 31 December 1990	27	-	27
Depreciation			
1 January 1990	11	-	11
Charge for year	2	-	2
31 December 1990	13	-	13
Net book amount			
31 December 1990	14	-	14
31 December 1989	16	-	16

The impact was a loss of £20.5m before tax for 1991 and a restatement of the 1990 results to show a reduced profit of £7.9m as a result of writing off development expenditure and product registration costs against the profit and loss account rather than capitalising them.

There is obviously some debate about whether R&D expenditure meets the normal definition of an asset. Clearly it only does it if it leads to the creation of a saleable product. But R&D is not the most unusual example of capitalising items, as the following examples, all of which are taken from companies in receivership or administrative receivership, seem to illustrate:

Exhibit 10.11 **Musterlin 1989 Report & Accounts**

Note 11 TANGIBLE FIXED ASSETS
(a) The Group

	Archive £000	Book Properties £000	Leasehold Improve- ments £000	Other Assets £000	Total £000
COST OR VALUATION					
At 31 December 1988	877	6,557	260	1,159	8,853
On acquisition of subsidiary	-	-	-	66	66
Additions	32	2,296	24	489	2,841
Disposals	-	-	-	(166)	(166)
At 31 December 1989	909	8,853	284	1,548	11,594
DEPRECIATION					
At 31 December 1988	14	1,350	-	450	1,814
On acquisition of subsidiary	-	-	-	60	60
Charge for year	17	697	30	210	954
Disposals	-	-	-	(136)	(136)
At 31 December 1989	31	2,047	30	584	2,692
NET BOOK VALUE					
At 31 December 1989	878	6,806	254	964	8,902
At 31 December 1988	863	5,207	260	709	7,039

(i) Included in additions to book properties is an amount of £250,000 (1988 £155,000) in respect of interest capitalised. Cumulative interest capitalised is £641,000.

(ii) Cost of book properties includes work in progress with a value of £1,285,000 (1988 £669,000). This is not depreciated.

(iii) The archive includes £515,000 (1988 £515,000) arising from a 1981 revaluation. This is not depreciated. The historic cost of the archive at 31 December 1989 was £339,000 (1988 £362,000).

(iv) Other assets include vehicles and equipment held under finance leases with a cost of £628,000 (1988 £375,000) and depreciation of £269,000 (1988 £197,000). Depreciation charges in the year were £109,000 (1988 £47,000).

Musterlin, a publisher, included Book Properties (i.e. books which it had bought publication rights to) as tangible fixed assets with a value of £6.8m out of total tangible fixed assets of £11.6m, and Capital and Reserves of £11m.

Sharp & Law, a shopfitting company, capitalised computer software products which were *to be* sold externally, i.e. that had not already been sold.

Exhibit 10.12 **Sharp & Law Accounts Annual Report 1988**

Intangible assets

Development costs in respect of computer software products to be sold externally are amortised over the estimated life of the product, at an annual rate of not less than 25 per cent.

Arguably another unusual example of capitalisation of costs by a major company is Cable & Wireless, which capitalises some employee costs:

Exhibit 10.13 **Cable & Wireless – Report & Accounts 1990**

Note 6. Employees

(a) The average weekly number of persons employed by the Group during the year was:

	1995 Number	1994 Number
Hong Kong	16,191	16,042
Other Asia	1,019	977
United Kingdom	10,248	10,086
Other Europe	416	477
Caribbean	7,719	8,041
North America	2,164	2,205
Rest of the world	3,183	3,275
Corporate centre	78	134
Associated companies	106	111
	41,124	41,348

(b) The aggregate remuneration and associated costs of Group employees, **including amounts capitalised, were:**

	1995 £m	1994 £m
Salaries and wages	793.4	722.7
Social security costs	39.8	34.1
Pension costs	66.6	57.8
	899.8	814.6

So-called 'hi tech' stocks are a potential minefield for capitalisation issues. A good example is provided by the fall from grace of Quality Software Products (QSP), a supplier of accounting software. QSP was floated in March 1993 at 380p per share and rose to a peak of over 700p as a result of the boom in technology stocks in 1995/96. However, shortly after a rights issue late in 1995 it issued a profits warning which caused a collapse in the share price which halved in just two days:

Figure 10.1   Quality Software Products share price 1993-96

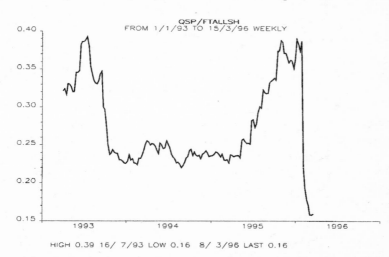

HIGH 0.39 16/ 7/93 LOW 0.16 8/ 3/96 LAST 0.16

Whilst the ostensible reason for the profits warning was delays in signing contracts, QSP was vulnerable to any setback in sales of its products because of its policy of capitalising development expenditure:

Exhibit 10.14   **Quality Software Products 1994 Annual Report**

Research and development
Research and development expenditure is written off as incurred, except that development expenditure incurred on an individual project is carried forward when its technological feasibility is reasonably established and the commercial viability can be foreseen with reasonable assurance. Capitalisation of development expenditure ceases when the products derived from the project are completed and fully tested. Any expenditure carried forward is amortised, using the 20% reducing balance method based on the estimated useful lives of the related products generated from the project with amortisation commencing in the period the product is available for sale. As required by SSAP 13, if circumstances dictate, expenditure considered to be irrecoverable is written off immediately.

This policy of capitalising development costs as an asset led to intangible assets from this source totalling £13.65m in 1994:

Exhibit 10.15   Quality Software Products 1994 Annual Report

INTANGIBLE FIXED ASSETS

	Development expenditure *£*
Cost:	
At 1 January 1994	
Increase during the year – own costs	15,926,629
– sub contract costs	5,536,872
	386,409
At 31 December 1994	**21,849,910**
Amortisation:	
At 1 January 1994	5,824,674
Provided during the year	2,374,575
At 31 December 1994	**8,199,249**
Net book value at 31 December 1994	**13,650,661**
Net book value at 1 January 1994	10,101,955

Development expenditure represents direct costs, salary costs and directly attributable overheads incurred in developing the OLAS and Universal OLAS range of products.

This clearly made the company vulnerable to any setbacks: shareholders' funds were only £15m so that a write off of the capitalised development expenditure as an expense would virtually wipe out the capital base.

Neither do companies which are involved in building or buying property assets restrict themselves to capitalising just interest expense. The restated 1991 profit figures given in the Queens Moat Houses 1992 annual report are explained as follows:

Exhibit 10.16   Queens Moat Houses Annual Report 1992

Capitalised expenses. The group had previously capitalised certain expenses in connection with certain hotels including interest, pre-opening marketing expenses, professional fees and maintenance wages. Your board considers that such expenditure should not be capitalised. Accordingly, the assets have been written off, with the result that pre-tax profits have been reduced in 1991 by £21.9 million.

11

BRAND ACCOUNTING

Another chance for the UK accountancy profession to indicate to the world that it has utterly failed to get its act together!
Neil French, Finance director of APV, formerly with Touche Ross, describing Brand Accounting in *Financial Weekly*, 12 April 1990

OF BIDS AND DEALS

Brand Accounting has its genesis in takeovers, mainly within the food manufacturing and processing, and drinks industries. On the one hand, placing a valuation on brands was seen as a defence against a takeover 'on the cheap'. On the other, predators who had acquired companies with brand names but few tangible assets found in brand valuation a way to make their balance sheet look better, and to overcome some technical problems caused by the intangible nature of brands. The result is a total lack of consistency in comparing companies which possess consumer brands.

Brands accounting really is a recent phenomenon. Its history is to be found in deals such as the 1978 bid by Allied Breweries for J. Lyons at a price which was considered too high by conventional yardsticks, but gave Allied control of J. Lyons' brands. Hanson's battle with United Biscuits for control of Imperial Group in 1986 gave Hanson the ability to sell off brand name food operations such as Golden Wonder and Ross to leave the tobacco interests at a net cost of only some £197 million for a business (Imperial Tobacco) which produced operating profits of £240m in 1991 (see Table 11.1).

Conventional wisdom had required break up bids for poorly run companies to come out at below asset value in order to achieve a profit for the predator. These bids suggested that the stock market was not valuing brand assets correctly.

Much of brand accounting's origins lie in the rival bids launched in 1988 by Nestlé and Jacobs Suchard, the Swiss confectionery groups, for Rowntree. Rowntree possessed valuable brands such as Kit-Kat, Quality Street, Polo, After Eight and Yorkie. Its shares were trading at 477p before the bid, compared with the final winning bid from Nestlé of 1075p per share.

Table 11.1   Hanson–Imperial break-up

			£m
1986	Acquisition	Imperial	2,500
	Sale	Hotels etc	–186
	Sale	Beer	–1400
	Sale	Crisps	–87
1987	Sale	Finlay	–19
	Sale	Bonds	–4
	Sale	Corners	–3
1988	Sale	Food	–335
	Sale	Food	–199
	Sale	Distribution	–9
1989	Sale	Food	–25
	Sale	Hardy	–9
	Sale	Food	–7
	Sale	Food	–20
	Residual cost		197

Ignoring: capital tax
acquired debt
retained profits

During the knock–down, drag-out fight which a contested bid becomes, many defences were used against the Nestlé/Suchard bids, including the fact that Nestlé and many other Swiss companies were protected from foreign takeover by their shareholding structure. Another was that the bid seriously undervalued Rowntree's brand names.

Merger and acquisition has continued as a potent driving force behind the development of brand accounting. In the first instance, as for Rowntree, this is because a potential victim wishes to establish the value of its brand to prevent a predator getting them 'on the cheap' since they were not reflected in the company's balance sheet net asset value. A good example is Cadbury Schweppes, with brands in confectionery and soft drinks, which faced stake building by the US company General Cinema at the time of the Rowntree bid. Cadbury Schweppes' 1989 Accounts introduced the value of brands acquired since 1985 including Trebor and Bassett at cost, thereby doubling shareholders' funds with over £300m of intangible assets. By doing so Cadbury also reduced its stated gearing.

Secondly, the intangible nature of brands has presented problems for acquisitive companies in the food and drinks industry which purchase companies whose main assets are their brands. In particular, if a company has significant brands it is likely to be taken over at a premium to net asset value which will leave the acquiror with substantial goodwill financed by borrowed funds.

Grand Metropolitan brand accounting

Grand Metropolitan has adopted an accounting policy whereby significant brands, acquired since 1985, the value of which is not expected to diminish in the foreseeable future, are recorded in the balance sheet as fixed intangible assets. No amortisation is provided on these assets but the value is reviewed annually by the directors and the cost written down as an *exceptional item* where permanent diminution in value has occurred.

As at 30 September 1995, Grand Met's brands were included in the balance sheet at £3,840m. This compares with shareholders' funds of £3,103m and net borrowings of £3,511m. Therefore balance sheet gearing on a published basis amounts to 113 per cent and this rises to infinity if the intangible brand names were written off.

In fairness it is worth stressing that the brand names do have value, albeit somewhat difficult to determine. Grand Met had interest cover of 5.3 times despite the high level of capital gearing, ex tangibles, in that year. Its return on equity was around 18 per cent in the last reported year so it appears to be making an adequate return on its intangible assets.

Brand valuation is a common problem in food and drink industry takeovers:

Table 11.2   Food and drink industry takeovers

Acquiror	Target	Goodwill as a percentage of price paid %
Nestlé	Rowntree	83
Grand Met	Pillsbury	86
Cadbury Schweppes	Trebor	75
United Biscuits	Verkade	66

It also produces problems with the Stock Exchange Listing Agreement (or 'Yellow Book') which measures the permissions which a company must obtain for an inquisition in part by reference to the acquiror's shareholders' funds, which may be quite small in relation to its market capitalisation (and that of its target), and requires a Class 1 circular and an EGM for quite small acquisitions.

Exhibit 11.1 **Cadbury Schweppes 1989 Financial Review**

Historically we have written off goodwill arising on an acquisition consequently reducing shareholders' funds. Intangibles – goodwill and brand values – have not been recognised in the Balance Sheet. In 1989 the International Stock Exchange introduced new rules for assessing the value of the Company's assets in relation to acquisitions and disposals which eliminated the discretionary right of the Stock Exchange to recognise the value of intangible assets unless they are shown in the accounts. This affects their assessment of the level at which circulars to shareholders, and possibly extraordinary general meetings, are required.

Consequently, we have included in our Balance Sheet the values of major brands acquired since 1985 at cost. We have decided that no amortisation is necessary as our accounts reflect significant expenditure in support of these brands, principally by advertising and sales promotion. The values will be reviewed annually and reduced if a permanent diminution arises. Our auditors have reviewed the basis and calculations of the brand values included in the balance sheet and endorse this approach.

ACCOUNTING FOR INTANGIBLES

There is no separate accounting standard for brand accounting – the initiative having originated in industry rather than the accounting profession. But brand accounting is currently governed by ED52 – 'Accounting for intangible fixed assets', although a Discussion Paper on "Goodwill and intangible assets" was issued by the ASB in June 1995. ED52 maintains that an intangible fixed asset should only be recognised in the balance sheet if:

(1) the historical costs associated with the asset are known or ascertainable,

(2) the characteristics of the asset can be clearly distinguished from goodwill and other assets, and

(3) its cost can be measured independently of goodwill and other assets.

It is evident from this that ED52 did not envisage the capitalisation of brand or other intangible assets 'created' from scratch within a business rather than acquired, when it may be possible to identify separate characteristics (1) − (3) above. Nonetheless one company stood out as having adopted brand accounting for brands created rather than acquired − Ranks Hovis McDougall (now part of Tomkins).

Exhibit 11.2 **Ranks Hovis McDougall Annual Report and Accounts 1989**

Intangible Assets

The accounting treatment for additions to goodwill is considered on an individual basis and elimination against reserves has been selected as appropriate for the current year.
Brands, both acquired and created within the Group, are included at their 'current cost'. Such cost, which is reviewed annually, is not subject to amortisation.

Note 13. Intangible Assets

	The Group 1989 £m	The Company 1989 £m
Brands		
At 3 September 1988	678.0	-
Additions	27.1	-
Disposals	(1.1)	-
Revaluation	36.0	-
At 2 September 1989	740.0	-

The Group has valued its brands at their 'current use value to the Group' in conjunction with Interbrand Group plc, branding consultants.

The basis of valuation ignores any possible alternative use of a brand, any possible extension to the range of products currently marketed under a brand, any element of hope value and any possible increase of value of a brand due to either a special investment or a financial transaction (e.g. licensing) which would leave the Group with a different interest from the one being valued.

The criteria in ED52 were clearly restrictive showing that it viewed the inclusion of brands in the balance sheet as undesirable. It rejected the idea of homegrown brands being in the balance sheet as the historical costs associated are unknown (RHM). It also rejected the policy of turning all potential goodwill from an acquisition into an intangible asset (Grand Metropolitan, Guinness, Cadbury Schweppes).

INTERBRAND'S APPROACH TO BRAND VALUATION

Market leader Interbrand Group assists companies to calculate the earnings directly attributable to the brand and multiplies this by an earnings multiple which is determined by the assessed strength of the brand based on its stability.

$$\text{Brand Valuation} = \star \text{ Brand Earnings}$$
$$(\text{where } \star = \text{the multiple applied})$$

Brand earnings are calculated from the net profit minus profits from own label manufacture. This figure is then manipulated in two ways: firstly figures for the last x years are used and restated at present values, and then a weighted factor is applied to reflect the importance of each year's profits. Often they use the last three years with a weighting of ½ to the present year, ⅓ to last year and ⅙ to the year before that. Note also that future profits are not taken into account, so a declining brand name will be overestimated in value and a growing brand name understated.

The resultant figure could over-estimate the asset value, as much of the value should be attributable to the other assets employed such as tangible fixed assets and management as well as the brands, and therefore could result in double counting on the balance sheet.

The multiple applied is derived from a mark given out of 100. The mark is based on the brand's strength in seven areas, where strength is defined by reliability; each area is weighted in order of importance. These are:

* *Leadership*
  Marks are given for its perceived influence on its market, its ability to resist competitive 'attacks' and its market share.

- *Market*

  Value of a brand is highly correlated with the market it operates in so consumer brands will score better than production brands. Areas prone to fashion changes will also receive a low rating.

- *Internationality*

  International brands are less affected by competitive attack in a particular country and by changes in its economic climate. Also a brand that is capable of crossing cultures and overcoming competition from foreign domestic firms is going to be more stable and therefore valuable.

- *Trend*

  The long-term earnings trend gives the view of the brand's future stability and prospects.

- *Investment*

  A brand which has received high advertising spending which is of high quality generally is a better quality brand.

- *Protection*

  Marks are also given for trade marks and patents dependent on their width and length, for example a patent for a drug such as aspirin with a wide range of pain-killing applications would be more valuable than a patent for a drug specifically to alleviate toothache.

The brands are valued at current cost although it is continually stressed that the valuation is not meant to be the estimated cost of the brand to develop or the total of the future discounted cashflows.

But even where brand accounting was adopted within the framework of ED52 i.e. for acquired brands, there are still problems. Probably the greatest is that where a company after an acquisition assigns a value to intangible assets such as brands rather than goodwill, it avoids having to apply either of the treatments required for goodwill, namely writing it off against reserves or amortising it over a period by a depreciation charge to the profit and loss account. Consequently, the brands are shown in the balance sheet without the profit and loss account bearing any charge for maintaining their value, unlike any other fixed asset (except sometimes land and buildings). As companies usually claim, the substitute for this is advertising and marketing expenditure to maintain the value of the brand:

Exhibit 11.3 **Cadbury Schweppes 1989 Accounts**

n) Intangibles

Intangibles represent significant owned brands acquired since 1985 valued at historical cost. No amortisation is charged as the annual results reflects significant expenditure in support of these brands but the values are reviewed annually with a view to write down if a permanent diminution arises.

Note 13. INTANGIBLES

	Group 1989 £m
Cost at beginning of year – as restated	104.3
Exchange rate adjustments	17.5
Additions	185.6
Cost at end of year	307.4

The restatement arises as a result of the change in accounting policy on intangibles.

Moreover, when companies claim that they do not need to depreciate brands since their advertising and marketing spend is intended to maintain the value of the brand, there is an obvious problem in that they are not obliged to reveal this cost item whereas the depreciation charge has to be declared and can therefore be compared for the same company over time or between companies in the same industry. Companies often hide behind the fig-leaf of 'commercial confidentiality' when asked about their advertising and marketing spend. One wonders whether some of the companies who are so vociferous in defending the lack of a depreciation charge for brands because of this maintenance expenditure are the same companies which lobbied for the proposals for disclosure of so-called 'revenue investment', such as advertising spend, to be dropped from FRED 1 which became FRS 3.

There is no substitute for a stated deprecation policy in attempting to achieve consistency between companies in their treatment of fixed assets.

Other problems are hinted at by Guinness's explanation of its policy on brands:

Exhibit 11.4 **Guinness Report and Accounts 1995**

BRANDS

The fair value of businesses acquired and of interests taken in related companies includes brands, which are recognised where the brand has a value which is substantial and long term. Acquired brands are only recognised where title is clear, brand earnings are separately identifiable, the brand could be sold separately from the rest of the business and where the brand achieves earnings in excess of those achieved by unbranded products.

Amortisation is not provided except where the end of the useful economic life of the acquired brand can be foreseen. The useful economic lives of brands and their carrying value are subject to annual review and any amortisation or provision for permanent impairment would be charged against the profit for the period in which they arose.

Guinness's policy is therefore to recognise brands where:

1. The title is clear – this would exclude a lease on a brand such as Whitbread's on Heineken, or Compass' fast food brands,

2. Brand earnings are separately identifiable – so that sales, costs and overheads must be known for each individual brand,

3. The brand could be sold separately from the rest of the business – implying a value purely on its own merits, and

4. The brand achieves earnings in excess of unbranded products – a brand of baked beans such as Heinz would have no value if it could not command greater earnings than supermarkets' own label products.

It is rare for an asset to be able to satisfy all of these criteria including separately identifiable earnings and the ability to be sold separately from the rest of the business. How many of the brands in the following table are truly separable from the business acquired with them?

Table 11.3   Brand accounting

Company	Main brands
Cadbury Schweppes	Sunkist, Bassett, Gini, Oasis, Canada Dry, Trebor
Grand Metropolitan	Burger King, Pillsbury, Smirnoff
Guinness	Johnnie Walker, Gordons, Bells
Ladbroke	Hilton
Reckitt & Colman	Colmans, Weslite, Dettol Airwick, Lemsip, Mr Sheen
United Biscuits	Callard & Bowser, Verkade
WPP	J Walter Thompson, Hill & Knowlton, Ogilvy & Mather

There is also a wider concern about comparability. One must suspect that Marks and Spencer and St Michael are two of the strongest consumer brand names in the UK, and although they were not acquired and therefore were not capitalised as brands under the terms of ED52, it is also likely that Marks & Spencer would not have felt the need to do so even if it were permissible. The complete absence of brand valuations from some consumer companies' balance sheets does raise an even bigger problem of comparability than the lack of amortisation on brand value. Unilever does not capitalise brands, unlike the other food manufacturers shown in the Table on Brand Accounting. Ladbroke included the value of the Hilton name in the Accounts whereas Forte did not include the value of its name. None of the brewers has followed Guinness's example.

There is now an ASB discussion paper on Goodwill and intangible assets. The main impact of this paper is likely to be on how companies treat goodwill, which is covered in Chapter 16. It also allows separate recognition of purchased brand values in a way similar to ED 52. There is a presumption that goodwill including brand values should be amortised or depreciated via an annual charge to the profit & loss account in line with the practice in most other countries. However, the discussion paper would allow companies not to amortise, but to conduct an annual 'impairment review' and to only write down the value of the intangible asset if it has been permanently impaired.

Given that virtually no companies wrote down the value of brands during the recession, despite most already having a policy of regular reviews and a probable fall in the value of brands such as the spirits companies brands or advertising agency names, the impairment review alternative proposed by the discussion paper looks like an option for companies to engage in a cop-out.*

* The only example of a brand value being written down which springs to mind is Perrier, where the write down was due to finding traces of benzene in the water.

12

CHANGES IN DEPRECIATION POLICY

**Q. What would aviators have thought about BAA's policy of
depreciating runways over 100 years a century ago in 1896?
A. Not a lot. There were no aeroplanes in 1896.**

Changes in depreciation methods, periods and policies have long been a
favourite source of manipulation of published profits. But why must
companies charge depreciation in the first place?

SSAP12

Depreciation is defined in SSAP12, published in 1977, as 'the measure of the
wearing out, consumption or other reduction in the useful life of a fixed
asset whether arising from use, effluxion of time or obsolescence through
technological or market changes'. It is worth noting that it is intended as a
measure of consumption, not a measure of change in value. SSAP 12
requires depreciation of all fixed assets except investment properties,
goodwill, development costs and investments.

The most commonly used method of depreciation is the straight line
method, followed by the reducing balance method (in various guises), the
annuity method and the unit of production method. A great deal of
discretion is left to the management in the choice of depreciation method,
as SSAP12 states: 'There is a range of acceptable depreciation methods.
Management should select the method regarded as most appropriate to the
type of asset and its use in the business so as to allocate depreciation as fairly
as possible to the periods expected to benefit from the assets' use.'

A change in the method of depreciation is only allowed if the new
method will better represent the company's results and financial position.
But a change of method is not a change of accounting policy, and profits can
be adjusted without even adopting a change of method, simply by altering
the life of an asset over which a method is applied.

CHANGE OF USEFUL ECONOMIC LIFE

The useful economic life is the period over which the owner expects to benefit from the asset, and once it, a residual value and a depreciation method have been arrived at, a depreciation charge can be calculated.

BAA (British Airports Authority) has made two significant changes in depreciation lives:

Table 12.1 BAA – useful economic life of certain assets

Year to 31 March	1988	1989	1990
Terminal lives (years)	16	30	50
Runway lives (years)	23.5	40	100

Exhibit 12.1 **BAA 1989 Report & Accounts**

Depreciation

No depreciation is provided in these Group financial statements in respect of freehold or long leasehold (leaseholds with an unexpired term of over 50 years) investment properties or land.

Short leasehold properties are depreciated over the period of the lease.

In the case of other assets, depreciation is calculated to write down the cost of these assets to their residual values on a straight line basis. The following table sets out the Group's standard term for each asset category:

Terminals	30 years
Runways, taxiways and aprons	40 years
Airport plant and equipment including runway lighting	15-25 years
Motor vehicles and office equipment	Over useful life which in most cases is 4-8 years
Furniture and fittings	5 years

A review carried out during the year of the useful lives of various airport assets has resulted in a revision in the case of terminals (previously depreciated over 16 years), runways (previously 23.5 years) and furniture and fittings (previously charged to the profit and loss account on a replacement basis). In addition, aircraft pavement maintenance expenditure previously capitalised is now charged to the profit and loss account as incurred.

The effect of the reassessment of useful lives of fixed assets and maintenance expenditure incurred during the year has not had a material effect on profit before tax but expenditure of £16.2m capitalised in prior years has also been charged in this year's financial statements.

Exhibit 12.2 **BAA 1990 Report and Accounts**

(d) Depreciation

No depreciation is provided in these Group financial statements in respect of freehold or long leasehold (leaseholds with an unexpired term of over 50 years) investment properties or land. Short leasehold properties are depreciated over the period of the lease.

In respect of other assets, depreciation is calculated to write down the cost of these assets to their residual values on a straight line basis.

It is the Group's policy to maintain certain properties occupied by Group members in a state of good repair so the residual values exceed the costs of these properties in the Group's accounts. As a consequence, no depreciation is provided on these properties.

The following table sets out the Group's standard term for each asset category:

Terminals	50 years (but see below)
Runways, taxiways and aprons	100 years
Airport plant and equipment including runway lighting	15-25 years
Motor vehicles and office equipment	Over useful life which in most cases is 4-8 years
Furniture and fittings	5 years

As part of a continuing review carried out in respect of the useful economic lives of its airport assets, the Group has reassessed the lives of terminal buildings (previously depreciated over 30 years) and runways, taxiways and aprons (previously 40 years) in the light of recent technological advances and an increasing volume of relevant historical data.

In respect of terminals, certain components have a life shorter than the life of the main structure. These components which were previously written off over the life of the terminals are now depreciated over a period of 10-20 years.

In the case of runways, taxiways and aprons, major periodic maintenance expenditure continued to be charged to the profit and loss account as incurred.

What is the significance of these changes? During this period, 1989-91, BAA undertook the following projects:

1. Terminal 3 Heathrow development – cost £110m

2. Heathrow runway resurfacing – £11.5m

3. Gatwick runway resurfacing – £6.5m

4. Gatwick refurbishment of South Terminal baggage and check-in systems – £22m

5. Stansted – new terminal – £395 m

6. Glasgow Airport terminal refurbishment – £47m

No depreciation was, of course, provided on the assets under construction during this period:

Exhibit 12.3 BAA 1991 Report and Accounts

Notes on the financial statements

11 Tangible fixed assets

(a) Airport assets

The movements in the year in airport assets were as follows:	Terminal complexes £m	Other freehold properties £m	Airfields £m	Sundry plant and equipment £m	Assets in the course of construction £m	Total £m
Cost						
Balance 1 April 1990	940.9	69.8	209.8	133.2	344.8	1,698.5
Reclassification	(14.9)	10.7	(11.5)	(3.6)	1.1	(18.2)
Transfers from non-airport investment properties (note 11b)	-	4.9	-	-	11.6	16.5
Additions at cost	356.9	14.1	49.9	59.0	(149.8)	330.1
Amounts capitalised	-	-	-	-	54.5	54.5
Disposals at cost	(9.2)	(0.3)	(0.3)	(2.4)	-	(12.2)
Balance 31 March 1991	1,273.7	99.2	247.9	186.2	262.2	2,069.2
Depreciation						
Balance 1 April 1990	290.6	0.2	74.6	77.2	-	442.6
Reclassification	(9.9)	-	(8.2)	(0.1)	-	(18.2)
Charge for the year	34.7	0.3	4.1	14.6	-	53.7
Disposals	(6.9)	-	(0.2)	(2.0)	-	(9.1)
Balance 31 March 1991	308.5	0.5	70.3	89.7	-	469.0
Net book cost 31 March 1991	965.2	98.7	177.6	96.5	262.2	1,600.2
Revaluation surplus	-	699.7	-	-	-	699.7
Total airport assets	965.2	798.4	177.6	96.5	262.2	2,299.9
Net book cost 31 March 1990	650.3	69.6	135.2	56.0	344.8	1,255.9
Revaluation surplus	-	767.0	-	-	-	767.0
Total airport assets	650.3	836.6	135.2	56.0	344.8	2,022.9

Once they emerged from construction, the assets were depreciated in accordance with the longer economic lives – the largest capital expenditure, Stansted's new terminal building, was completed in March 1991. It is not possible to give an accurate picture of the effect on BAA's profits, even though all the assets are depreciated on the straight line method, because the estimated residual values are still unknown. But clearly a move from 16 to 50 years economic life for terminals over two years with £574m of terminal work authorised or under construction makes a substantial difference. The 1990 Report and Accounts estimated that the effect on *current year* profits of those depreciation changes was a reduction of £8.6m if the changes had *not* been introduced. This amounted to just 3.4 per cent of 1990 pre-tax profits. But the impact on future profits should grow in line with expenditure on the assets.

The sums involved are smaller for runway resurfacing, but it is worth bearing in mind with a shift in estimated economic life from 23.5 to 100 years that 100 years ago man had not achieved powered flight. So will BAA be deriving economic benefit from aircraft using its runways in 2096?

CHANGES OF LIFE AND METHOD

Exhibit 12.4 **Cable & Wireless Report and Accounts 1990**

(d) TANGIBLE FIXED ASSETS AND DEPRECIATION

Depreciation of tangible fixed assets is set aside on the basis of providing in equal annual instalments for the cost or valuation over the estimated useful lives of these assets, namely:

Telephone cable and repeaters	up to 25 years
Landlines	20 to 40 years
Freehold buildings	40 years
Leasehold land and buildings	up to 50 years or term of lease if less
Plant	2 to 33 years
Cableships	up to 30 years

Depreciation provided on capital projects relating to major network development is calculated by reference to network usage as a proportion of expected usage when the network is complete.

The provision of depreciation on the basis of usage means that part of Mercury's depreciation charge has become a variable cost growing in line with usage in later years of the project. Cable & Wireless is far from being the only company to use the unit of production or usage method of depreciation. It is most frequently used in the mineral extraction and oil and gas industries when depreciation is linked to estimated depletion of the assets:

Exhibit 12.5 **BP Annual Report and Accounts 1989**

Depreciation

Oil, coal and mineral production assets are depreciated using a unit-of-production method based upon estimated proved reserves. Other tangible and intangible assets are depreciated on the straight line method over their estimated useful lives.

In 1988, depreciation of Cable & Wireless's major network developments was changed to a unit of usage basis. Annual depreciation is calculated by comparing the network usage to the estimated total usage over the estimated life of the network. This method prevents a high depreciation charge in the early years of the network's life when usage may not have built up and losses may therefore be declared after depreciation, or at least, profits depressed. The main potential problem is of course estimating usage over the full economic life of the network. If this is overestimated then the unit of usage charge in the early years will be too low, thereby storing up trouble for later years when the network will be overvalued in the balance sheet and will need to be written down.

Cable & Wireless's other main move, in common with BAA, has been to extend the lives of digital exchanges from ten to 15 years.

This change was not evident for the Cable & Wireless Report and Accounts:

Exhibit 12.6 **Cable & Wireless Report and Accounts 1987**

(d) TANGIBLE FIXED ASSETS AND DEPRECIATION

Depreciation of tangible fixed assets is set aside on the basis of providing in equal annual instalments for the cost or valuation over the estimated useful lives of these assets, namely:

Telephone cable and repeaters	up to 25 years
Landlines	20 to 40 years
Freehold buildings	40 years
Leasehold land and buildings	up to 50 years or term of lease if less
Plant	**2 to 33 years**
Cable ships	up to 25 years

During initial development of major capital projects depreciation is charged to accounting periods having regard to the utilisation of those assets.

Freehold land, where the cost is distinguishable from the cost of the building thereon, is not depreciated.

Certain land and buildings are included at open market value for existing use.

Surpluses and deficits on disposals of tangible fixed assets are determined by reference to sale proceeds and revalued net book amounts.

Cable & Wireless Report and Accounts 1990

(d) TANGIBLE FIXED ASSETS AND DEPRECIATION

Depreciation of tangible fixed assets is set aside on the basis of providing in equal annual instalments for the cost or valuation over the estimated useful lives of these assets, namely:

Telephone cable and repeaters	up to 25 years
Landlines	20 to 40 years
Freehold buildings	40 years
Leasehold land and buildings	up to 50 years or term of lease if less
Plant	**2 to 33 years**
Cableships	up to 30 years

Depreciation provided on capital projects relating to major network development is calculated by reference to network usage as a proportion of expected usage when the network is complete.

Freehold land, where the cost is distinguishable from the cost of the building thereon, is not depreciated. Certain land and buildings are included at open market value for existing use.

In previous years furniture, fittings and motor vehicles were written off in the year of acquisition. It is considered that this treatment is no longer appropriate and these items are now capitalised as plant. The previous year's amounts have been restated. The adopting of this policy in previous years would not have had a significant effect on profits for these years. Surpluses and deficits on disposals of tangible fixed assets are determined by reference to sale proceeds and revealed net book amounts.

Digital exchanges evidently fall within the category of 'Plant' where depreciation lives vary from two to 33 years.

Referring to the accounts of the subsidiary concerned, Mercury, produces more detail, but still not sufficient to identify the change in depreciation lives:

Exhibit 12.7   Mercury Communications Limited Report and Accounts 1987

(c) Tangible fixed Assets and Depreciation

Depreciation of tangible fixed assets is set aside on the basis of providing for their cost over their estimated useful lives. During initial development, depreciation of assets forming part of the communications network is charged to accounting periods having regard to the utilisation of those assets. Depreciation of other assets is provided in equal annual instalments.

The estimated useful lives of the assets are:

Communications Network	
Fibre optic cable, ducting and plant	10 to 40 years
Microwave plant	8 to 20 years
Earth station plant and equipment	10 to 20 years
Terminal equipment	**5 to 15 years**
Other plant and equipment	3 to 10 years
Short leasehold property	Over the terms of the lease
Rights of use	Over the term of the agreement

Mercury Communications Limited Report and Accounts 1991

Tangible fixed assets and depreciation

Depreciation of tangible fixed assets is set aside on the basis of providing for their cost over their estimated useful lives. During initial development, depreciation of assets forming part of the communications network is charged to accounting periods having regard to the utilisation of those assets. Depreciation of other assets is provided in equal annual instalments.

The estimated useful lives of the assets are:

Communications Network	
Fibre optic cable, ducting and plant	10 to 40 years
Microwave plant	8 to 20 years
Earth station plant and equipment	10 to 20 years
Terminal equipment	5 to 15 years
Other plant and equipment	3 to 10 years
Digital Switches	**15 years**
Short leasehold property	40 years or over the terms of the lease if less
Rights of use	Over the term of the agreement

The 1987 accounts for Mercury show Terminal equipment lives estimated at five to 15 years. But by 1991 a separate category for Digital Switches with estimated lives of 15 years had been identified. It would be difficult to determine the change in depreciation lives from this information.

The effect of the change was to reduce the rate of growth in the depreciation charge at a time of heavy capital expenditure on digitalisation by Hong Kong Telecom and Mercury. Also in March 1990, the life of cable ships was extended from 25 to 30 years. The move on digital exchanges, for example, from ten to 15 years cut the depreciation charge on these items by a third. But, as ever, it is necessary to ask 'Does it matter?' and if so 'How do I spot a change in depreciation life or method?'.

THE EFFECT ON EARNINGS

To suggest that there is something intrinsically right or wrong in depreciating digital exchanges over ten or 15 years is to miss the point. It is equally difficult and probably irrelevant for us to determine whether unit of usage is a more appropriate method of depreciation for major network developments than the straight-line method.

What is important is to be aware of the impact on profits of a change from one method or period to another. The table shows Cable & Wireless's five year profits record, adjusted for the change in depreciation policies. The lower pre-tax profits which result from adjusting to reflect the previous depreciation policies would be directly reflected in Earnings per Share since the actual tax charge would be unaffected, as depreciation is not a tax allowable expense. The average growth in profits over the five-year period has been inflated by 2½ per cent p.a. from 14.3 per cent to 16.7 per cent by the depreciation policy changes:

Table 12.2   Cable & Wireless – Adjusting for depreciation charges

Year to 31 March	1985	1986	1987	1988	1989	1990	Five year average growth %
Reported							
Pre-tax profit	245.2	295.0	340.5	356.1	420.5	526.7	+16.7
Tax charge (%)	30	27	22	18	18	18	
EPS (p)	15.8	19.3	22.0	24.0	27.9	31.3	+14.7
Adjustments							
Depreciation							
Actual	92.4	88.0	88.9	99.5	118.7	195.7	
Adjusted	92.4	105.4	116.6	132.7	174.2	250.3	
Difference	–	-17.4	-27.7	-33.2	-55.5	-54.6	
Adjusted pre-tax profit	245.2	277.6	312.8	322.9	365.0	472.1	+14.3

Source: Cable & Wireless Report and Accounts

This is important in assessing the correct rating for the shares – it is just as painful to lose money by buying an overvalued share which falls in price as it is to lose the same amount of money buying shares in a company which fails because of creative accountancy. Moreover, such accounting changes can create a treadmill effect for a company: if there are no further changes in accounting policy, Cable & Wireless's profits will have to grow 2½ per cent p.a. faster over the next five years to match the *reported* profits growth in 1985–90. The expectation of this profits growth to match the historic performance may well be discounted in the share price, given the dangerous tendency for investment analysts to extrapolate from the past in compiling forecasts, which may prove disappointing if organic profits growth does not move up a gear to replace the impetus previously provided by accounting changes.

HOW TO SPOT IT?

Obviously, close attention to the Accounting Policy notes in the Annual Accounts is necessary to spot changes in depreciation methodology, although it is worth remembering that a change in depreciation method is *not* a change in the accounting policy and does not therefore have to be noted as a change in accounting policy notes. Although the new method or period for depreciation will usually be shown in the accounting policy notes, attention may not be drawn to the change by a specific note, so careful attention has to be given to comparing the Accounting Policies with the previous year's notes.

Changes in depreciation policy can also be derived by comparing depreciation with the assets in the business to determine whether the proportion of total assets depreciated each year is changing over time:

Table 12.3   Cable & Wireless – Depreciation over a five-year period

	1985	1986	1987	1988	1989	1990
Depreciation charge (£m) (A)	92	88	89	100	119	196
Average gross assets (£m) (B)	1036	1182	1307	1489	1953	2806
A/B %	8.9	7.4	6.8	6.7	6.1	7.0

Source: Cable & Wireless Report and Accounts

Between 1985 and 1990, Cable & Wireless's depreciation charge fell from 8.9 per cent p.a. of the assets employed to 7.0 per cent. These trends can also be compared with industry competitors to determine whether they represent an industry-wide trend or whether a company's depreciation policy is moving out of line with others in the same business:

Table 12.4 Depreciation/Average Gross Assets (%)

UK	1986	1987	1988	1989	1990
British Telecom	7.5	8.8	9.3	8.9	9.4
Cable & Wireless	7.4	6.8	6.7	6.2	7.0
Racal Telecom (now Vodafone)	10.5	10.6	11.1	10.0	9.9
USA					
AT&T	9.9	9.4	9.2	8.3	
MCI	10.3	9.3	9.6	10.1	
Sprint	13.7	13.2	11.2	10.9	
United Telecom	7.3	8.3	10.3	8.5	
Ameritech	7.7	7.8	7.3	7.3	
Bell Atlantic	8.6	9.4	8.9	8.5	
Bell South	6.5	7.3	7.1	7.0	
Nynex	7.0	8.5	7.9	7.9	
Pacific Telesis	7.1	7.7	7.7	7.4	
Southwestern Bell	6.5	7.3	7.5	7.5	
US West	6.9	7.4	7.4	6.7	

Intercompany comparisons suffer from some disadvantages, such as the different age profiles of the companies' assets, different asset mixes and the fact that the US regional Bell Telephone companies are regulated for the most part by return on assets. Nonetheless there is a clear discrepancy between Cable & Wireless's percentage depreciation/assets at 7.0 per cent and the average for the rest of the industry.

These methods of detecting the impact of changes in depreciation policy are doubly important because policy changes are often implemented *before* completion of major capital expenditure, such as BAA's Stansted terminal, or Cable & Wireless's investment in digital exchanges, so that the impact on profits of a change in policy may not be readily apparent simply from the Accounting Policy change and is only revealed by the sort of calculations shown above.

UITF ABSTRACT 14

This UITF Abstract implements from December 1995 a new rule that the (material) impact of changes in accounting policy, including those on depreciation, should be shown for both the current accounting period and the prior period. Whilst this is a step forward in bringing to investors' attention the impact of accounting policy changes, there are still some drawbacks. As the prior examples make clear, companies are adept at changing depreciation methods just before the depreciation charge on a new asset would have a substantial effect on profits. Moreover, a change in say the length of the depreciation period remains outside the definition of a change in accounting policy, so that its impact would still not need to be quantified under UITF Abstract 14.

DEPRECIATION OF PROPERTY

In recent years a situation has arisen in some companies' treatment of property assets for depreciation purposes which has some common features with the debate about brand accounting. In particular, a number of companies have stopped depreciating some or all of their properties which are held on freeholds or long leaseholds. Properties held on short leases obviously have to be depreciated in value over the remaining life of the lease.

Most of the companies involved have been holding property assets in the hotel and leisure industries:

Exhibit 12.8 **TRAFALGAR HOUSE ANNUAL REPORT**

Depreciation is not normally provided on freehold and long leasehold hotels and properties owned and occupied as business premises. It is the Group's policy to maintain its properties in a sound state of repair and, accordingly, the Directors consider that the lives of the properties are so long and residual values are at such a level that depreciation is immaterial. Other properties held as fixed assets are stated at valuation.

Exhibit 12.9 **SCOTTISH & NEWCASTLE DEPRECIATION**

Freehold licensed, non-industrial and leisure properties are not depreciated, it being group policy to maintain them to such a standard that the estimated aggregated residual values are at least equal to their book values. Other properties are depreciated over their estimated useful lives of 40 to 50 years.

In the case of Forte the properties are mainly hotels, as they were until recently at Trafalgar House with its ownership of the Ritz and other hotels. Scottish & Newcastle not only has pubs, including Chef & Brewer which it bought from Grand Met, but also the Center Parcs holiday villages.

Nor have hotel and other companies restricted themselves to omitting to provide depreciation solely on buildings:

Exhibit 12.10   **Queens Moat Houses 1991 Annual Report**

Depreciation and repairs and maintenance

The group had previously not depreciated its fixtures, fittings, plant and equipment. Your board consider this to have been inappropriate. Moreover, certain repairs and maintenance expenditures were also being capitalised. Provision has now been made in the profit and loss account for depreciation of fixtures, fittings, plant and equipment and relevant repairs and maintenance expenditure is being expensed. This policy change has reduced net assets in 1991 by £2.5 million and reduced 1991 pre-tax profits by £50.9 million

---

In every case where depreciation is not provided, the accounting policies talk about repair and maintenance spending maintaining the value of the properties. This may be so, but allowing companies not to depreciate properties raises the same sort of problems as brand accounting. Since no stated policy of depreciation is applied we cannot be sure that any usage of the property is not reducing its value without debiting a depreciation allowance to the profit & loss account before a profit is struck. Refurbishment and maintenance spend is not separately identified in accounts in the way that depreciation is to enable us both to calculate what proportion of the property's value a company is spending each year, and to gauge whether this seems reasonable both in the absolute and in comparison with other companies in the same industry. Without a standard imposing some form of depreciation and a statement by the company about how this is calculated, there is no hope of ensuring consistency in measuring results.

There is a strong suspicion that in some cases this lack of desire to apply a depreciation charge has been driven by the poor results which the hotel industry has shown, particularly through the recession. Hotel companies have shown very low profit returns compared with the value of their hotel assets, so that even quite a gentle depreciation charge on these large asset values would wipe out a significant proportion of profits.

The ASB has now decided to reverse this stance, and require depreciation of all properties.

13

TRANSFER FROM CURRENT TO FIXED ASSETS

A long-term investment is a short-term investment which went wrong.
Investment adage

This is an old saying in stockbroking which was reflected in the behaviour of a number of companies during the recession, particularly since amongst the characteristics of the recession was a fall in property values accompanied by a near total absence of liquidity to enable developers to realise properties, even if they were prepared to accept the fall in values and the inevitable loss.

Property developers rely upon selling the buildings they develop. Even if the building is tenanted, the developer usually still needs to sell. Unlike the property investor who arranges equity and long-term debt finance, a property developer is typically funded partly by short-term bank debt which needs to be repaid from the sale of the property. Indeed, in many cases, developers cannot even cover their loan interest without regular disposals.

In a very real sense therefore a property developer's buildings are his stock-in-trade, and a company is required to show its stock in its balance sheet at the lower of cost or market value. If the stock should fall below cost, the result is that it would be forced to show a loss which would appear in the profit & loss account in the same way as a profit over and above cost on the sale of stock would appear.

The same is of course not true for fixed assets. A company does not generally trade in its fixed assets. So instead of being valued at the lower of cost and realisable value, they are included in the balance sheet at historic cost less any depreciation (although just to confuse the issue, property assets are sometimes subject to periodic revaluations). Even if the market value drops below the balance sheet value derived by this method, there is no requirement to show any fall in the value of fixed assets through the profit & loss account since they are not held for re-sale.

This presented an opportunity for companies, such as property developers, who saw a sharp fall in the value of their stock below cost level during the recession. They found that they could avoid the resulting loss passing through the profit & loss account if they transferred the asset from current assets to fixed assets prior to writing it down.

Exhibit 13.1 **Ladbroke Group – 1990 Annual Report and Accounts**

Note 12. Investment Properties

Held for development, third party renting and capital appreciation	Total	Freehold cost or valuation	Long leasehold cost or valuation	Short leasehold valuation
	£m	£m	£m	£m
At 31st December 1989	757.7	695.8	61.6	0.3
Exchange rate movements	(58.0)	(56.2)	(1.8)	-
Net additions (c)	118.7	93.9	25.0	(0.2)
Revaluation surplus	(105.9)	(97.8)	(8.1)	-
At 31st December 1990	**712.5**	**635.7**	**76.7**	**0.1**
Representing assets states at:				
Valuation (a)	646.3	575.4	70.8	0.1
Cost (b)	66.2	60.3	5.9	-
At 31st December 1990	**712.5**	**635.7**	**76.7**	**0.1**

(a) Valued by property division directors or a professional executive of the company, following consultation with external professional advisers, or by independent external valuers, on an open market basis. The property division directors were J Anderson, A P Grant, H Harris or P G Martin FRICS and the executive was J D Broughton ARICS.

(b) At cost in the course of development, the current value being estimated by the directors to be not less than the book amount.

(c) Net additions comprise additions of £205.1m including a transfer of £67.9m from dealing properties, freehold disposals of £86.2m and short leasehold disposals of £0.2m.

(d) The amount of investment properties determined according to the historical cost accounting rule, as at 31st December 1990, is £670.7m (1989 £566.2m) which includes capitalised interest of £113.6m (1989 £88.4m).

(e) Investment properties are accounted for in accordance with SSAP 19. Where the requirements of SSAP 19 have been followed as the directors believe this is necessary in order to present a true and fair view.

In 1990, Ladbroke transferred £67.9m worth of properties from dealing properties, which by definition are current assets, to investment properties as shown in note 12(c) of the accounts. Interestingly, in the same year the revaluation 'surplus' on investment properties was minus £105.9m. In other words the investment properties fell in value by this amount. It is a fair bet that some of this fall in value was due to the dealing properties which had been transformed into investment properties. Hence that old saying ' A long term investment . . . etc.' By taking any reduction in value in its dealing property portfolio in this way, Ladbroke might have avoided the problem of showing the loss through the profit & loss account on which most analysts and investors focus.

It might be argued that the net effect on the value of shareholders' investment in Ladbroke was the same however the write-down was taken. If it was taken through the profit & loss account then retained profits would be lower, so reducing shareholders' funds which were directly reduced by the same amount by the treatment which was actually adopted. This is the sort of technical argument from accountants which totally misses the point that presentation is all. Or as they say about jokes, its all in the way you tell them. With the stock market fixated with valuing companies on an earnings multiple, there is obviously a considerable potential penalty for a company which puts such a fall in value through its profit & loss account.

That the stock market has been poor historically at seeing through the antics of companies which inflate their profit performance at the expense of the balance sheet is shown by the Trafalgar House share price performance up to 1990.

Figure 13.1   Trafalgar House share price 1981–95

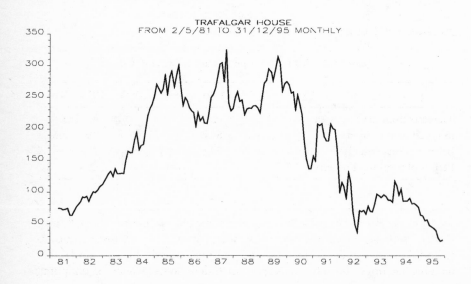

TRAFALGAR HOUSE
FROM 2/5/81 TO 31/12/95 MONTHLY

There is some justice in the fact that Trafalgar House should be one of the companies to fall foul of the UITF Abstract 5 Transfers from current to fixed assets: which simply specified that prior to a company transferring assets from the current to the fixed assets category, the transfer should be made at the lower of cost or realisable value, i.e. after any necessary write-down had occurred and had been taken to profit & loss account. The result was a restatement of Trafalgar House's profits sharply downwards:

Table 13.2 **TRAFALGAR HOUSE PUBLIC LIMITED COMPANY 1991 COMPARATIVES RESTATED**

Profit/ (Loss) for the year	£m
1991 Published Accounts	44.9
UITF 5 Property Write Down	(102.7)
FRRP -Act Written Off	(20.0)
UITF 3 Goodwill on Disposals W/O	(21.6)
1992 Published Accounts	**(99.4)**

A NEW TRICK: TRANSFERRING IT BACK

Most attention which has been focused upon this technique of 'creative' accounting has dwelt upon the transfer of assets from current to fixed assets prior to writing down the value. But the recovery from the 1990-92 recession has brought with it a new technique.

Table 13.3   AB Ports property transfer/write downs

	1990	1991	1992	1993	1994	Total
Transfers from development to investment property	85.1	81.8	–	-6.3	-0.6	160.0
Balance sheet write down	25.0	39.6	23.3	–	–	87.9
P&L profits on Inv Property	–	–	–	6.0	2.5	8.5

AB Ports has the apparently unusual distinction of having gained from switches between current and fixed assets in both directions. As well as its docks business, AB Ports has undertaken a number of diversifications including property development. This did not just relate to surplus land at its port facilities, but, for example, included development of shopping centres.

As the table shows, in 1990 and 1991 AB Ports transferred £85.1m and £81.8m respectively of development property to the investment property category. The table also shows that in the same period it took write downs of £25m and £39.6m on its investment properties. We have no way of knowing whether all of these write downs relate to the same development properties which had just been transferred, but the timing is propitious. Moreover, if some or all of the amounts written off do relate to the investment properties transferred I would have wanted to know at what value properties were transferred. If they were transferred at too high values, one reason could have been that it was done in order to protect the profit and loss account from the write downs. In any event, how else does one explain such a large write off within the year?

But what may be of more current interest are the profits from the sale of investment properties shown in 1993-94. This raises a new possibility, namely that the write downs to the balance sheet eventually depressed the book value of these properties below their market price, and the gain when they were sold was then taken to the profit & loss account. In some cases, the only figure that may ever have appeared in AB Ports profit & loss account for these developments is the profit on disposal, even though in reality the group has made a significant loss compared with the original cost before write offs. Try explaining that to the legendary Man on the Clapham Omnibus. This may not give an accurate view of the true economic performance of AB Ports property development activities in a way which would be familiar to the ordinary investor who occasionally buys and sells residential property.

So you see that investors cannot relax their vigilance even when companies are recovering from recession, since the techniques which moved losses into the balance sheet are capable of being reversed to move 'profits' on the same assets into the profit & loss account.

14

CURRENCY MISMATCHING

Business? It's quite simple. It's other people's money.
Alexander Dumas fils

INTEREST RATE ARBITRAGE AND TAX

The practice of borrowing money in low interest rate currencies and depositing it in high interest rate currencies became so prevalent in the 1980s and early 1990s, particularly amongst groups with substantial US and UK interests, that it even acquired a respectable name: interest rate arbitrage.

This is in fact a misuse of the term arbitrage. An arbitrage is the simultaneous purchase and sale of two equivalent securities between which an unsustainable price differential has arisen so as to generate a risk free profit. If a company has ordinary shares and convertible shares in issue, and you could convert into the ordinary shares at an effective price 10% below the ordinaries, investors would buy the convertible and short sell the equivalent number of ordinaries. They could then convert into ordinaries and deliver them to cover their short sale, thereby realising a profit.

Take a simple example. Imagine a company's ordinary shares cost £1, and each convertible costs 450p and converts into five ordinary shares. You could sell the ordinaries at £1 and then effectively buy them back at 90p (450p divided by 5). And if you buy at 90p and sell at £1 you make 10p profit even if you sell before you buy (which is what short sellers always do).

In order to make an arbitrage work it is necessary for it to satisfy two main conditions. 1) The securities must be equivalent. It may be no good, for example, if the securities cannot be converted for several years, or if there is an income differential so that the stock being sold carries a higher dividend yield than the one being bought; and 2) the buying and selling should be executed simultaneously otherwise there is a risk that the price of the other security will shift adversely. For example, if the convertible was purchased for 450p, but the price of the ordinary shares fell below 90p before they were sold, the so-called arbitrage would make a loss.

The term arbitrage is frequently misused. Genuine arbitrages sometimes occur in takeovers when one company offers its shares in exchange for those of another. For example, if Company A bids two of its ordinary shares for every three shares in Company B. If A's shares are trading at say 150p each and those of the target B are at 90p, you can buy two of A's shares for 300p. Once the bid is declared unconditional, A's and B's shares are about to become synonymous, so you could buy three of B's shares for 270p and sell the equivalent, two of A's shares, for 300p to make a profit. It is important that the bid is unconditional before you attempt to execute an arbitrage. Otherwise the differential in the share prices may just indicate that the bid is about to fail so that the two shares will not become the same security.

However, the concept of arbitrage was taken a step further by the invention of risk arbitrage. This involves buying shares in the target company before it is bid for. Apart from the fact that this is clearly not a risk free arbitrage, since the two shares cannot be the same if the bid has not yet even occurred, it was sometimes a cover for insider dealing as practised by Ivan Boesky and others.

Similarly, so-called interest rate arbitrage does not warrant the term arbitrage. One currency is rarely if ever a perfect substitute for another. Even where currencies are pegged within a fixed exchange rate mechanism, unexpected movements occur as sterling proved again in 1992 when it was forced out of the European Exchange Rate Mechanism. Indeed, the reason why differential interest rates exist between currencies and enable companies to make an interest margin by borrowing one and depositing the funds in another is precisely because the market expects the rate of exchange between the two currencies to shift. It is for this reason that companies frequently incur capital losses which more than offset the interest gains from this practice.

Neither is it possible for companies to obtain the interest benefit of currency mismatching and protect themselves against possible capital loss by hedging, for example, by taking out a forward foreign exchange contract to safeguard themselves against the possibility that the rate may move against them. In a perfect market, and the foreign exchange market is probably the best example of a perfect market, the cost of forward cover will remove any interest rate advantage. So companies which practise this form of arbitrage must leave their capital position uncovered, which as the example on page 122 shows, can prove costly. Anyone can get lucky for a time and not only reap the benefit of differential interest rates, but also guess the timing of when to open and close the position so as to avoid capital losses. But nobody guesses right all the time, and eventually, playing these games will usually result in capital losses, as a number of companies have demonstrated over time.

Just to add a twist to the tail of the interest rate 'arbitrage' game, some of the companies which have engaged in this pursuit have also managed to book the profits through tax advantageous routes. A bank deposit in sterling need not be held in the UK. A company which borrows US dollars in order to sell them and deposit the proceeds in sterling at a higher rate might choose to deposit the funds in an offshore tax shelter such as the Cayman Islands where the interest income is not taxable.

The result would be a subnormal tax charge in the group accounts, since the interest charged on the borrowing would earn tax relief but there would be no equivalent charge on the interest received. Hanson's tax charge has remained below the UK Corporation Tax rate for years, and hit a low point which coincided with the largest differential between US and UK interest rates:

Table 14.1 **Hanson tax charge**

	1984	1985	1986	1987	1988	1989	1990	1991	1992	1993	1994	1995
%	25.7	23.5	22.4	22.8	17.8	23.6	28.9	19.6	15.3	27.8	20.8	20.4

Hanson managed to report a tax charge below the UK Corporation Tax rate and that in its other main area of operations – America – for over a decade. How?

This highlights another clue to spotting currency mismatching and other techniques: if the tax charge is consistently low, why? This simple reason for raising questions was pointed out in the Survival Techniques chapter of the first edition, and it remains just as valid today.

WHY MISMATCH?

The advantages of currency mismatching lie in the boost which it can provide to profits, often at the expense of the balance sheet. To take an example, during the first half of 1991, UK interest rates were significantly higher than US dollar rates: average sterling LIBOR was 12.8 per cent versus an average US Prime Rate of 8.9 per cent. Borrowing funds in US dollars and depositing in sterling would on a simple basis seem to produce a positive interest margin of nearly four per cent which could be credited to profit and loss account.

Simple, isn't it?

CURRENCY TRANSLATION

But interest rate differentials between currencies exist for reasons other than to provide companies with net interest income from mismatching borrowings in one currency and deposits in another. They are intended to reflect differing inflationary expectations in the economies concerned and to express differences in the expected movements between currencies – so that potentially hard currencies carry lower interest rates, and softer currencies which are expected to depreciate on the exchanges carry higher rates to compensate for this. Consequently, the interest gain from currency mismatching can be more than wiped out by exchange losses.

Take the example of a company which at the end of 1990 decided to take advantage of the difference in UK and US rates by borrowing $193m, translating this into £100m at the ruling exchange rate of £/$1.93. How would it have fared in the first half of 1990?

Table 14.2 Mismatching: gain on the savings, lose on the roundabouts

	As at 31.12.90 £/$1.93	As at 30.6.91 £/$1.62
Deposit	£100m	£100 = $162m
Borrowing	$193m = £100m	$193m

The company should have earned a four per cent interest differential for six months, so that the effect of net interest income on its profit and loss account will be:

Interest income £100m @ 12.8% for 6 months =	£6.4m
Interest payable $193m @ 8.9% translated @ $1.78*	£4.8m
	£1.6m

* Average exchange rate

Not bad, £1.6m of net interest income for a company which had no cash of its own on deposit. The problems set in when the company goes to unwind the transaction and repay the borrowing from the deposit. Because the dollar has strengthened (there were only 1.62 dollars to the pound by 30 June versus 1.93 dollars six months earlier), the £100m deposit would translate into only $162m but the company has to repay $193m borrowing leaving it with a capital loss of $31m. Not such a good deal!

Of course the company may not need to repay the loan at that point, but still translation of the balance sheet assets and liabilities including the deposit and loan will produce the same unrealised loss which is taken to reserves. But herein lies the rub: the net interest income goes through the profit and loss account, but the exchange loss is taken through the balance sheet in accordance with SSAP20, as shown by BP's accounting policy notes and movements in reserve (see Exhibit 14.1).

Exhibit 14.1   BP Annual Report and Accounts 1989

Foreign Currencies

On consolidation, assets and liabilities of subsidiary companies are translated into sterling at closing rates of exchange. Income and source and application of funds statements are translated at average rates of exchange.

Exchange difficulties resulting from the translation at closing rates of net investments in subsidiary and related companies together with differences between income statements translated at average rates and at closing rates, are dealt with in reserves.

Exchange gains and losses arising on long-term foreign currency borrowings used to finance the group's foreign currency investments are also dealt with in reserves.
All other exchange gains and losses on settlement or translation at closing rates of exchange of monetary assets and liabilities are included in the determination of profit for the year.

Note 28. Reserves

Group reserves include undistributable reserves attributable to:

		£ million
	1989	1988
Parent company	10	10
Subsidiary companies	2,019	1,626
Related companies	392	414
	2,421	2,050

Included in group reserves are amounts retained by overseas subsidiary and related companies which may be liable to taxation if distributed.

Exchange adjustments for the year include unrealised losses of £15 million (£% million profit) on long-term foreign currency borrowings.

As a consolidated income statement is presented a separate income statement for the parent company is not required. The profit for the year of the group dealt with by the parent company and the reserves of the parent company are as follows:

		£ million
	1989	1988
At 1 January	2,601	2,234
1987 final dividend to former Britoil shareholders	-	(9)
Shares purchased from KIO	(2,423)	-
Profit for the year	2,105	1,199
Distribution to shareholders	(795)	(823)
At 31 December	1,488	2,601

POLLY PECK INTERNATIONAL

Polly Peck reported a net interest credit in its accounts to December 1989 despite having begun and ended the year with significant net debt. The figures are shown in the table below:

Table 14.3   Polly Peck – Net borrowings/interest

£m	Beginning	1989 End	Average*	Interest	Implied rate %
Borrowings	377	1106	742	(55.6)	7.5
Bank deposits	124	300	212	68.1	32.1
Net debt	253	806	530	12.5	2.3

* This is the average of the year start and end debt figure, not necessarily the true average debt/cash for the year.

As the balance sheet only shows net debt at start of the year and the end and the group did not give an average net debt figure, we have estimated this by taking the average of these two figures. Polly Peck acquired Del Monte for £557m in December 1989 of which £280m was funded by a rights issue. If the net cash cost of Del Monte is taken off the year end debt figure of £530m, the implied interest rate on the debt of about £200m increases to around 9.2 per cent.

The difference between the interest rate achieved on deposits and that paid on debt can be caused by a number of factors:

1. The group had fixed low rate debt while cash was in deposits at variable rates which were currently high. In Polly Peck's case, the 1989 balance sheet showed guaranteed bonds (Swiss Francs and Dm) of £217.5m at rates between 5.75 and 6.25 per cent.

2. Significant swings in cash flow during the year which can result in the year end figure being substantially different from the average. Supermarkets, for instance, tend to have a regular cash inflow from customers, but pay their suppliers on a particular day of the month. Some businesses have a highly seasonal pattern, such as most retailers with a strong Christmas trade which gives them plenty of cash in a 31 December balance sheet.

3. A difference in the international spread of debt and deposits where

deposits are made in soft currencies at high interest rates, but borrowings are made in hard currencies at low rates.

The last factor is potentially very dangerous as, in the long run, soft currencies tend to depreciate against hard currencies resulting in currency losses. In Polly Peck's case, the 1989 accounts stated that a £10.5m provision was made in the Profit and Loss Account in respect of unrealised currency losses. In addition, the group made adjustments direct to reserves of £44.7m in 1989 and £170.3m in 1988 in respect of 'exchange variances on net investments overseas' – this item may have been affected by the international debt/cash position.

MATCHING CURRENCY AND ASSET LIABILITIES

There are circumstances in which no overall loss to a company, realised or unrealised, occurs – primarily where foreign currency borrowings are used to acquire assets in the same currency. In this case the appreciation in the value of the currency borrowing against sterling is equalled and cancelled out by the appreciation in the sterling value of the currency assets acquired.

But this does not mean to say that all companies which finance overseas assets with currency borrowings are exempt from the balance sheet effect of currency mismatching. Often a company concerned will use overseas operations to take on larger debt in the currency than its local assets in order to gain mismatch advantages. Probably one of the best examples recently is Beazer, which had US dollar borrowings representing 96 per cent of net debt based upon its Koppers acquisition. The adverse exchange movements on this debt in the first half of 1991 was one of the reasons which forced Beazer firstly to propose floating its European operations, and then into accepting a rescue takeover bid from Hanson.

HOW TO SPOT IT

How can an investor detect when a company may be mismatching currencies? The simplest method is to undertake the calculation shown above for Polly Peck – compare net interest income/expense with average deposits/borrowings shown in the balance sheet. If this produces an implied rate of interest which looks peculiar then the company *may* be mismatching. Take the example of Fisons:

Exhibit 14.2 Fisons Annual Report and Accounts 1989

Note 3. Finance income	1989	1988
	£m	£m
Interest payable in respect of loans and overdrafts:		
Wholly repayable within five years	(16.1)	(12.1)
Other	(3.2)	(2.3)
Interest receivable	21.3	17.4
Exchange gains	-	5.4
	2.0	5.4

Note 15. Creditors – amounts falling due after one year

	1989	1988
	£m	£m
Notes:		
(1) The aggregate amount repayable by instalments any of which are repayable beyond five years	2.3	2.0
(2) Details of loans other than from banks are:		
Repayable beyond five years		
Parent Company		
5⅞% Unsecured Loan Stock 2004-09	4.3	4.3
Fisons Finance Netherlands BV		
5¼% Guaranteed Convertible Bonds 2001: US$ 31,690,000		
(1988 – US$46,545,000)	21.9	25.7
	26.2	30.0
Repayable between two and five years:		
Fisons Finance Netherlands BV		
9% Guaranteed Notes 1994		
Kuwaiti Dinars 15,000,000	31.9	-

Included in prepayments is an amount of £0.6m (1988 $0.9m) in respect of bond issue expenses not yet written off.

	Net borrowings	
£m	1988	1989
6½% Debenture stock	6.2	-
Bank loans and overdrafts	50.0	33.7
Loans other than from banks	116.0	138.3
Finance leases	1.5	1.4
Loans and leases – amount due after one year	44.6	131.0
	218.3	304.4
Less: cash	151.8	189.9
Net borrowing	66.5	114.5

Average net borrowing £90.5m ((£66.5m + £114.5m) divided by 2).

Fisons' net interest income of £2m squares strangely with simple average net debt for the year of £90.5m. Obviously, this calculation carries all the normal caveats about using the balance sheets which only give a snapshot of opening and closing debt, but the implication of earning net interest *income* whilst carrying net *debt* poses some interesting questions, which may be partly answered by the glimpse of Fison's financing techniques given by Note 15 in the Accounts which shows borrowing in foreign currencies including exotica such as Kuwaiti dinars.

There are other reasons why this calculation can produce apparently impossible rates of interest. Nonetheless, this simple method raises questions which should have been sufficient to steer a wary investor clear of Polly Peck or Fisons.

As a 'screen' this is an effective method of raising questions about currency mismatching:

Table 14.4   1991   Net interest paid

Average net debt*

Company	Interest** paid £m	Interest received £m	Net interest £m	Average net debt £m	Implied† interest rate %
Grand Met	(305)	107	(198)	2748	(7.2)
Fisons	(361)	26	(10)	144	(6.9)
Hazlewood Foods	(16.6)	9.5	(7.1)	103.1	(6.9)
RTZ	(158)	108	(50)	739	(6.8)
Reed Intl	(65.3)	39.2	(26.1)	402.8	(6.5)
Blue Circle	(60.0)	37.0	(23.0)	373.5	(6.2)
Christian Salvesen	(3.0)	–	(3.0)	48.5	(6.2)
Ocean Group	(13.0)	10.0	(3.0)	54.5	(5.5)
Scottish & Newcastle	(36.0)	22.5	(13.5)	290.8	(4.6)
Shell T&T	(678)	630	(48)	1092.5	(4.4)
Smith & Nephew	(35)	32	(3)	75.5	(4.0)
British Gas	(224)	125	(99)	2997.5	(3.3)
Hays	(0.6)	–	(0.6)	21.5	(2.8)
Courtaulds	(44)	39	(5)	221.5	(2.3)
Vickers	(12.4)	12.0	(0.4)	22.0	(1.8)
Redland	(50)	51	1	238.2	0.4
Lasmo	(113)	116	3	800.5	0.4
Bowater	(57)	58	1	196	0.5
Storehouse	(15.7)	16.2	0.5	20.0	2.5
Marks & Spencer	(34.2)	47.5	13.3	351.5	3.8
Cable & Wireless	(53.0)	59.2	6.2	81.5	7.6
Johnson Matthey	–	3.4	3.4	40.0	8.5

Notes: * Average of year opening and year end debt. Convertible loan stocks treated as debt.

** Including interest capitalised.

† A cut off rate of approximately 7.0% implied rate paid has been taken.

( ) Implies interest rate paid.

Exhibit 14.3   **Hanson – 1991 Accounts**

Consolidated Balance Sheet

at 30 September 1991	1991 £m	1990 £m
Fixed assets		
Tangible	6,199	5,057
Investments	429	704
	6,628	5,751
Current assets		
Stocks	992	984
Debtors	1,192	1,126
Listed investments	6	5
Cash at bank	**7,765**	6,878
	9,955	8,993
Creditors: due within one year		
Debenture loans	1,725	20
Bank loans and overdrafts	810	2,041
Trade creditors	507	501
Other creditors	1,332	1,309
Dividend	377	355
	4,751	4,226
Net current assets	5,204	4,767
Total assets less current liabilities	11,832	10.528
Creditors: due after one year		
Convertible loans	500	-
Debenture loans	579	420
Bank loans	3,801	3,828
	4,880	4,258
Provision for liabilities	3,627	3,436
Capital and reserves		
Called up share capital	1,202	1,199
Share premium account	1,153	1,155
Revaluation reserve	163	163
Profit and loss account	807	317
	3,325	2,834
	11,832	10,528

Exhibit 14.3 (contd.)   **Hanson – 1991 Accounts (contd.)**

Assets and Liabilities by Currency

at 30 September 1991	Sterling £m	US Dollars £m	Total £m
Fixed assets			
Tangible	1,387	4,812	6,199
Investments	269	160	429
	1,656	4,972	6,628
Current assets			
Stocks	439	553	992
Debtors	587	605	1,192
Listed investments	1	5	6
Cash at bank	7,532	233	**7,765**
	8,559	1,396	9,955
Creditors: due within one year			
Debenture loans	358	1,367	1,725
Bank loans and overdrafts	639	171	810
Creditors and taxation	1,128	711	1,839
Dividend	377	-	377
	2,502	2,249	4,751
Net current assets	6,057	(853)	5,204
Total assets less current liabilities	7,713	4,119	11,832
Creditors: due after one year			
Convertible loans	500	-	500
Debenture loans	199	380	579
Bank loans	2,765	1,036	3,801
	3,464	1,416	4,880
Provisions for liabilities	710	2,917	3,627
	4,174	4,333	8,507
Shareholders' funds	3,539	(214)	3,325
	7,713	4,119	11,832

An easier guide to potential currency mismatching is simply to look for substantial *gross* short-term borrowings and deposits in the balance sheet even if the net debt or cash position is low. Although holding companies sometimes run borrowings in some subsidiaries and credit balances in others for reasons of local management autonomy, or because the balances are in different countries and provide a currency hedge by financing local assets, it is not always logical treasury management for a group to operate indefinitely with substantial borrowings and credit balances since it is then in essence borrowing its own funds back from the banking system with which they are deposited, and paying a margin for the privilege of doing so.

Hanson, which has had a high level of net interest income to average net debt shows in Exhibit 14.3: 1) cash at bank £7765m, and borrowings of £7415m (the debt figures are obtained by adding the individual items – see Table 14.5) at the end of 1991, and 2) in the breakdown of assets and liabilities by currency, the US dollar assets and liabilities have net borrowings of £2721m and negative shareholders' funds of £214m to suggest overborrowing in this currency, and sterling operations show net cash of £3.71bn. And of course this is a snapshot so that the mismatching may be greater between balance sheet dates. Net interest income of £188m in 1991 represented 14 per cent of pre-tax profits.

Exhibit 14.4 Hanson Report and Accounts 1991

Note 3. Costs and overhead less other income

	1991 £m	1990 £m
Changes in stocks of finished goods and work in progress	86	1
Raw materials and consumables	3,689	3,572
Employment costs (note 4)	1,216	1,107
Depreciation	210	172
Depreciation of finance leases	6	8
Profit on disposal of fixed assets	(22)	(11)
Other operating charges	1,565	1,349
Share of profit on associated undertakings	(20)	(43)
Profit on disposal of natural resource assets	(170)	(101)
Interest receivable	**(929)**	**(824)**
Interest payable (note 5)	**741**	**638**
	6,372	5,868

Other operating charges include hire of computers, plant and machinery £71m (£73m), remuneration of auditors £4m (£4m) and expenditure on research and development of £34m (£34m). Income from listed investments amounted to £12m (£32m).

The growth in Hanson's gross cash position is illustrated by figure 14.1.

Figure 14.1 Hanson's Gross Cash Position (£m)

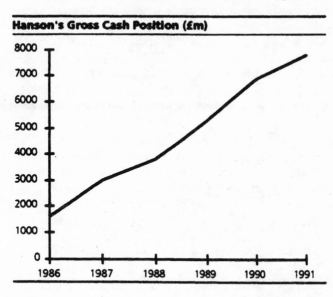

Moreover, when the currencies in which Hanson held its cash and debt is analysed, the picture become even clearer:

Table 14.5 Hanson Cash and Debt by Currency

Sept 30 1990	In Sterling	In Dollars	Total
	£m	£m	£m
Cash	£6425	£453	£6878
Debt	(£3220)	(£3099)	(£6319)
Total	£3205	(£2646)	£3559

Sept 30 1991	In Sterling	In Dollars	Total
	£m	£m	£m
Cash	£7532	£233	£7765
Debt	(£4461)	(£2954)	(£7415)
Total	£3071	(£2721)	£350

Table 14.5 shows that Hanson's net debt position of £2.6-£2.7bn in US dollars was very nearly matched by its net deposits in sterling of £3.0-3.2bn. If this is combined with the increasing gross cash position (i.e. the position before deducting debt) which Hanson was running, what does that tell us? That Hanson might have been using its US operations to gear up and then swapping the proceeds into sterling, so taking advantage of the differential between US and UK interest rates. This is also indicated by the steady build-up in the gross cash and debt balances: cash increased from £6.9bn in 1990 to £7.8bn in 1991.

Part III

Techniques Which the ASB is About to Change

15

PENSION FUND ACCOUNTING

The Great Illusion
– title of a book by Norman Angell, 1874–1967

How a surplus arises

The 1980s saw widespread announcements of overfunded pension schemes by UK companies. Of a survey of 100 of the largest companies by market capitalisation in the UK★, the median funding level was 125 per cent of the schemes' liabilities. In a similar survey in November 1990 only six out of 100 companies disclosed a funding level below 100 per cent.

A surplus arises when the actual valuation of a fund produces a figure greater than that required to meet the estimated liabilities to members of the fund. The valuation process by which this funding level is determined is far from straight forward, primarily because the actuary is dealing with pension liabilities which are by their very nature long-term, and he therefore needs to assess the long-term values of the assets held to meet these liabilities.

Moreover, the value of both assets and liabilities will change over time. Liabilities are affected by growth in the wage bill since most pension schemes (or 98 out of the 100 companies surveyed) have defined benefit schemes, where pension payments are linked to an employee's final salary. The company therefore has to ensure that the scheme has sufficient income to make these payments, and the actuary will have to estimate the wage inflation rate for employees of the company up to their date of retirement. Less important, but still a factor in estimating the scheme's liabilities, is the expected rate of inflation or as it is more usually called, indexation of the pensions paid to retired members of the scheme.

On the asset side, the valuation is not the process which most private investors would understand. The actuary does not look up the prices of shares held by the fund in the *Financial Times* and ask chartered surveyors for valuations of the fund's property assets etc. It is not a realisation value which is being sought, rather the investment return expected on the fund's assets

★ Bacon & Woodrow, *SSAP 24* Survey of Practice from Published Accounts, September 1991.

over the same time scale as its liabilities, in order to determine whether those returns are sufficient to cover its liabilities.

The valuation parameters which are usually quoted in the disclosure of actuarial assumptions are the investment return and salary increases. In some cases, assumed dividend increases rather than anticipated total investment returns are cited. Also in some cases the expected rate of indexation in pensions is given. In other examples only the difference in growth between investment returns and salary increases is given rather than the absolute figures, since this difference is the critical factor in determining the funding level.

A Bacon & Woodrow survey showed the net investment return (net of expected salary increases) for 91 companies:

Figure 15.1   Frequency chart of assumption for interest net of pay increases

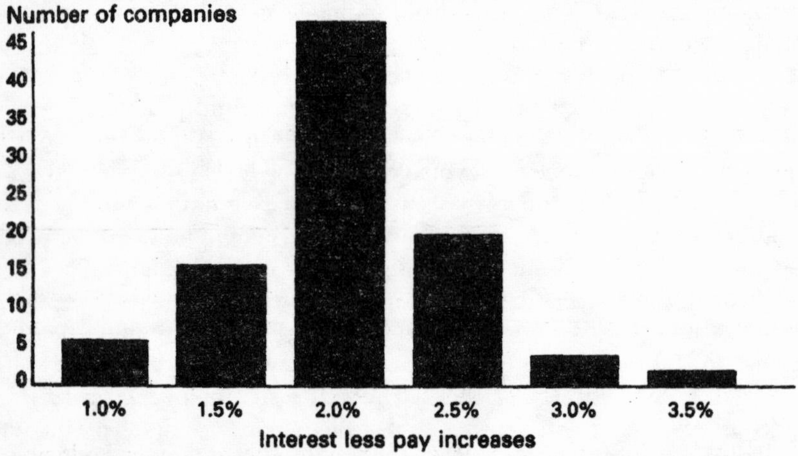

Source: Bacon & Woodrow

The net investment return assumptions range from 1 to 3½ per cent, but the majority are around two per cent.

So how do pension fund surpluses arise? 1) Investment returns greater than anticipated, and/or 2) wage increases which are lower than expected. Or, to put it more bluntly, by previous actuarial assumptions on these factors proving to be too pessimistic, so that the contributions which a company has been required to pay into the fund have proved excessive.

In the 1980s in particular, investment returns in UK equities were exceptional during the long bull market, and easily outpaced wage inflation; a situation which has not deteriorated in the 1990s with the onset of low inflation.

Table 15.1 Net investment returns in the 1980s

%	1980	1981	1982	1983	1984	1985	1986	1987	1988	1989	1990	1991
Total return on UK Equities	35.0	13.5	28.9	28.8	31.6	20.6	27.6	8.0	11.6	36.0	-9.7	20.7
Wages & salary inflation	18.6	7.5	6.6	6.8	6.7	8.8	8.7	8.8	11.5	11.3	10.8	5.0

Most funds are revalued triennially, and by the mid 1980s investment returns were clearly outstripping wage inflation so that surpluses were built up. This process was given a big boost at the beginning of the 1980s by the labour shake-out which occurred in UK manufacturing industry during the 1980-81 recession, which helped to produce fund surpluses since it is inflation in the total wage bill which accounts in the valuation of the fund, and reductions in headcount clearly relieve this pressure on fund liabilities.

ACCOUNTING FOR A SURPLUS – SSAP 24

SSAP 24 was introduced in May 1988 with the aim of introducing a systematic basis for reporting the impact on companies of the pension fund surpluses which were becoming increasingly important. Prior to the introduction of SSAP 24, the generally accepted practice in the UK was to charge pension costs in the profit and loss account on the basis of actual payments made to the fund i.e. on a cash basis, which obviously caused wide fluctuations in the impact on profits as overfunded schemes arose from triennial valuations and some contributions ceased.

SSAP 24 aimed to spread the charge to profit and loss account for the pension fund contribution over the period in which the company receives benefit from the employee's services i.e. an accrual concept. The Standard explicitly separated this from the funding or cash flow concept.

SSAP 24 gave companies with a pension fund surplus a choice to account either by reorganising the surplus as a balance sheet item and create a prepayment asset as a prior year item, or by spreading the benefit of the surplus forward in its profit and loss account over the remaining service life of the scheme's members. Since the second of these two methods is by far the most popular method of dealing with a surplus under SSAP24 we will examine this first.

HOW TO TREAT A SURPLUS

1. Spreading

Once a surplus has been identified by one of several actuarial valuation methods, the benefit of the surplus is spread over the remaining service life of the employees. This sounds simple enough, but even the method of spreading can significantly affect disclosed profits. But first, what is the effect of spreading a surplus?

(i) reduced pension and fund contributions If spreading of the surplus results in a variation from the regular cash contribution to the fund required by the actuarial valuation of assets and liabilities and projected growth rates. This surplus is credited to the profit and loss account once it has been spread by one of the several methods (see below) and will result in the reduction or even elimination of the charge for pension fund contributions for a time.

(ii) negative pension cost Where a surplus is large enough, the surplus spread over the remaining service lives may be larger than the regular annual cost, which can result in a credit to the profit and loss account as shown in the WH Smith example (Exhibit 15.1). Smith showed a regular cost of £18.2m for 1991 compared with a variation arising from spreading the pension fund surplus of £29.4m. This obviously made it unnecessary for the regular cost of £18.2m to be debited to profit and loss account in the period, and furthermore the excess of £11.2m was credited to profit and loss account.

These treatments of a pension fund surplus give rise to a number of problems:

(a) Method of spreading a surplus
There is currently no one accepted method of spreading a surplus although this may be about to change, and different methods produce different impacts over time. Spreading over the average service life of the work force

requires first an estimate of the *average* length of service remaining until retirement age, taking into account deaths, retirements, resignations and redundancies. This average will usually be shorter than most people imagine. As Table 15.2 shows, it can vary from about six to 15 years.

Exhibit 15.1   W H Smith Annual Report 1991

Note 25. Pension costs

The Group operates a number of pension schemes. The major schemes, which cover over 90% of members, are of the defined benefit type and are contracted-in to the State Earnings Related Pension scheme ('SERPS'). The assets of the schemes are held in separate funds administered by trustees.

The most recent formal actuarial valuations of the schemes were undertaken as at 31 March 1988 adopting the attained age method. The market value of the assets of the UK schemes was £311.8m and the actuarial value of the assets was sufficient at that date to cover 129% of the benefits that had accrued to members after allowing for expected future increases in earnings. The principal actuarial assumptions used for the valuations were as follows:

Investment return	9.0% pa compound
General increase in earnings	7.5% pa compound
Pensions increase	4.0% pa compound

The surplus of the actuarial valuation of assets over the benefits accrued to members is being eliminated by a reduction in employer contributions.

The pension cost relating to the UK schemes has been assessed in accordance with the advice of a qualified actuary based on the same actuarial valuations, updating them to 1 June 1991. The pension cost charged in the profit and loss account is as follows:

Major UK Schemes	52 weeks to 1 June 1991 £m	52 weeks to 2 June 1990 £m
Regular cost	18.2	15.3
Variation from regular cost	(29.4)	(19.3)
	(11.2)	(4.0)
Other schemes	-	0.3
Credit for the period	(11.2)	(3.7)

The variation from regular cost for the period represents the amortisation of the estimated surplus at the beginning of the period spreading it by equal instalments of capital and reducing elements of interest over the estimated service lives of the existing members taken as 9 years. The pension costs relating to overseas schemes are immaterial.

The social security costs shown in note 24 above include SERPS contributions of approximately £3.5m (1990 – £3.2m).

Once this estimate is established, a method of spreading the surplus over this period must be applied. Three commonly applied methods are: 1) the straight line method, 2) the mortgage or fixed amount method and 3) the percentage of pensionable pay method.

Take the example of a fund with a surplus of £7m spread over eight years. An estimated investment return of nine per cent and payroll inflation of eight per cent would produce the following variation in annual surplus:

Table 15.2   The three spreading methods

Year	Straight line £000	Fixed amount £000	Percentage of pay £000
1	1385	1160	930
2	1310	1160	1000
3	1235	1160	1065
4	1165	1160	1145
5	1090	1160	1220
6	1020	1160	1310
7	945	1160	1400
8	875	1160	1500
Total	9025	9280	9570

The straight line method is calculated by dividing the surplus of £7m by the number of years service to give a level capital amount per annum of £875,000. Interest is added to the unamortised balance each year to give the total charge. In common with the other methods, this produces a total figure which exceeds the original surplus because of the necessity to include an interest element, since the actuarial surplus itself is a discounted amount or net present value of future flows.

The mortgage or fixed amount method calculates a fixed annuity which would provide the surplus of £7m plus interest in line with the investment return of nine per cent p.a. in the fund. As in mortgage repayments, the annual surplus can be regarded as comprising mainly interest with a small capital element at the outset and vice-versa in later years.

The percentage of pay method is calculated by taking a stream of payments increasing each year at the same rate as the estimated rate of payroll inflation used in valuing the fund (seven per cent).

It can be seen that the methods produce very different impacts upon the profit and loss account, with the straight line method taking the bulk of the benefit of the surplus 'up front' and the percentage of pay method reversing this. This problem is compounded by the fact that companies are not disclosing the method of spreading utilised so that it is impossible to draw comparisons even between two companies with exactly the same pension surplus situation.

b) How should earnings from pension fund surpluses be valued?
Using a pension fund surplus to reduce or eliminate employer's contribution to a pension fund is an increase in earnings since it reduces or eliminates the regular charge in the profit and loss account. But how should this source of earnings be valued? This can be a significant question: the W H Smith pension fund surplus in 1991 eliminated a regular cost of £18.2m. Even ignoring the surplus over and above this amount also credited to profit and loss account of £11.2m, this will have boosted pre-tax profits by 25.7 per cent to £89.0m, plus a further 18.8 per cent for the amount of negative pension cost credited to profit and loss account. Combined this represents nearly a 50 per cent increase in Smith's profits excluding these items.

The most obvious problem with earnings generated from this source is their substantiality. It must be accepted that earnings from this source cannot be guaranteed because future triennial revaluations could throw up deficits rather than surpluses. This happened in the 1970s when wage inflation last outstripped investment returns. Indeed, in a sense the current surpluses only arose in part at least because past actuarial valuations were too pessimistic about investment returns versus wage inflation, including the inability to predict the massive headcount cuts and investment returns which helped to produce the surpluses. Why is it impossible that current valuations are too optimistic?

Moreover, the benefit of the surplus will diminish, the rate depending on the method of spreading used. But clearly a company using the straight line method will have a lower benefit in later years. A simple way of looking at this is to ask what PER would a company attract if its only earnings were these annual pension fund reductions in regular cost? Pretty low, I would suggest, if the benefit diminishes over time, and even lower given that the surplus could disappear completely or be transformed into a deficit at the next triennial valuation.

Without further upward revision in the surplus, a pension fund surplus credit to profit and loss account will naturally reverse in due course, and the company will revert to charging the full annual cost to profit and loss account. This is indeed the whole purpose of SSAP 24: to make the surplus disappear by means of an annual credit to profit and loss account. If the surplus is amortised over eight years, then in year nine the company will revert to charging the full regular cost in the profit and loss account which will cause a quantum leap in costs for a company with the size of annual surplus reduction of W H Smith.

Table 15.3   Estimated rundown of W H Smith pension fund credit

Year	1	2	3	4	5	6	7	8	9	10
£m										
Amortisation of surpluses										
– capital	16	16	16	16	16	16	16	16	16	–
– interest	13.4	11.6	10.2	8.7	7.3	5.9	4.4	3.0	1.5	–
	29.4	27.6	26.2	24.7	23.3	21.9	20.4	19.0	17.3	–
Less: Regular cost	(18.1)	(19.7)	(21.6)	(23.7)	(26.0)	(28.5)	(31.3)	(34.3)	(37.6)	(41.2)
P&L credit (debit)	11.2	7.9	4.6	1.0	(2.7)	(6.6)	(10.9)	(15.3)	(20.1)	(41.2)

To illustrate the point, the Table above gives an estimate of the run down in the effect of W H Smith's pension fund surplus. The notes to the Accounts indicate that it has been spread using the mortgage method, as shown above. The assumptions are: an investment return of nine per cent p.a. on the fund in line with the actuarial assumptions, wage growth of seven per cent p.a. (ditto) and two per cent p.a. growth in staff numbers in line with the physical expansion of Smith's operations. The surplus is amortised over nine years, in line with Smith's practice.

The result is interesting. By year five the credit to profit and loss account has reverted to being a charge, and there is a leap in this charge in year ten as the surplus has been fully utilised. Any investor who placed the same multiple on Smith's profit and loss credit in year one from the pension fund as on its other earnings would have a nasty shock later.

c) Negative pension cost
The W H Smith example has already shown a fund in which spreading the surplus produces a negative pension cost i.e. a credit to profit and loss account, in the first year. This arises where the amortised surplus exceeds the regular cost. This could occur, for example, where the pension fund surplus is so large that it cannot be eliminated over the average working life of the

scheme members by reducing the profit and loss account charge to zero, or where a company is using a front-end loaded method of spreading the surplus such as the straight line method.

There is no reason within SSAP 24 why this 'negative cost' should not be recognised. It does of course give rise to a prepayment asset in the balance sheet. But it is necessary to be aware of the nature of this item. It is a non-cash element of profits i.e. the pension fund does not pay the company anything to match this negative cost so that counting it as part of normal earnings can give a misleading impression of the company's cash generation. And the balance sheet asset formed by this credit has limited usefulness – it can be used to increase employees' pension fund rights but is not freely available for use in the business.

This reflects the fact that despite the philosophy of SSAP 24, which is that a defined benefit pension fund is a vehicle for the company and that any surplus is regarded as a company asset, and any shortfall in provision of the defined benefits would have to be made up by the company, there are very few cases of companies succeeding in getting a cash repayment from an overfunded scheme. Hanson tried and failed with the Imperial Group scheme, although this was complicated by the fact that Hanson had disposed of most of the operating businesses covered by the scheme. Probably the most significant success recorded is Lucas' cash refund of £90m from a £560m surplus.

But all these examples are rare – generally a pension fund credit to profit and loss account which exceeds the regular cost is a non-cash credit and should be treated accordingly. Whether or not a surplus can be realised by the company in cash depends on the exact terms of the trust deed under which the scheme is run, but examples are rare.

2. *Prior year adjustment*

In the year of implementation of SSAP 24 the Standard permits an alternative method to that of spreading a surplus (or deficit) across the average working lives of the members of the scheme: the incorporation of the surplus or deficit into the balance sheet by a prior year adjustment, creating a prepayment asset (if a surplus) or an accrual (if a deficit). This is a different treatment to an asset which may be created because a pension fund surplus spread over the life of schemes' members exceeds the regular annual cost, thereby causing a 'negative cost' or credit in the profit and loss account, which will give rise to a prepayment asset in the balance sheet. In addition, some prepayments may arise in a company's balance sheet simply because the company has paid into the pension fund earlier than required. An example is given by Marks & Spencer:

Exhibit 15.2 **Marks & Spencer 1990 Annual Report**

Note 16. Debtors	Group		Company	
	1990	1989	1990	1989
	£m	£m	£m	£m
Amounts falling due within one year:				
Trade debtors	47.9	47.1	19.4	22.6
Amounts owned by Group companies	-	-	472.2	293.3
Groups funds utilised in financial services (see note 14)	46.3	-	-	-
Other debtors	43.4	35.7	37.2	26.6
Prepayments and accrued income	81.9	81.1	71.2	70.0
	219.5	163.9	600.0	412.5
Amounts falling due after more than one year:				
Advance corporation tax recoverable on the proposed final dividend	40.9	34.7	40.9	34.7
Deferred taxation provision arising on short-term timing differences	(21.6)	(23.1)	(18.4)	(20.1)
	19.3	11.6	22.5	14.6
Other debtors	17.9	17.1	17.8	16.7
	37.2	28.7	40.3	31.3
	256.7	192.6	640.3	443.8

Trade debtors include advances to suppliers of £6.7 million (last year £12.4 million) against bills of exchange drawn on the Company in respect of merchandise to be delivered between April and September 1990.

Other debtors include loans to employees, the majority of which are connected with house purchases. These include a loan to an officer of the Company, the balance of which amounted to £8,112 at 31 March 1990 (at date of appointment £9,120). Transactions with directors are set out in note 26 on page 74.

Prepayments and accrued income include £50.6 million in respect of the UK pension scheme for 1990/91 (last year £52.1m in respect of 1989/90).

The decrease in the Group's provision for deferred taxation of £1.5 million (last year increase of £1.5 million) is represented by a credit to the profit and loss account of £2.1 million (last year charge of £0.6 million) and exchange movements of £0.6 million (last year nil).

Although creation of a prepayment asset for a pension fund surplus is within SSAP 24's terms, investors need to be aware of its existence and the effect on key financial ratios:

Exhibit 15.3 **Williams Holdings Report and Accounts 1990**

Note 18. DEBTORS

	Group		Company	
	1990	1989	1990	1989
	£000	£000	£000	£000
Trade debtors	90,744	139,624	173	104
Pension fund repayment (note 28)	72,820	76,465	-	-
Amounts owed by subsidiary companies	-	-	224,552	280,064
Other debtors	16,900	18,199	670	1,818
Prepayments and accrued income	6,050	8,697	462	1,033
Corporation tax net recoverable	37,982	30,376	48,800	29,931
	224,586	273,361	275,657	312,950

Note 28. PENSIONS

The group operates pension schemes for the majority of employees in Europe and North America. The larger schemes are of the defined benefit type, and costs are assessed with the advice of a qualified actuary using the projected unit method. For the purposes of assessing excess funding and contributions, the principal actuarial assumptions are based upon an investment return of 10% per annum, pay growth of 7% per annum and dividend growth of 5.5% per annum. These assumptions have been used to standardise the basis of pension costing throughout the group and may differ from those used by trustees of individual schemes. The resulting net excess funding of **£72,820,000** (1989 £76, 465,000) has been included in debtors and the profit and loss account credit for £3,338,000 (1989 £1,514,000) is net of interest accrued on the surplus. The change in the net excess funding in the main arises from the Crown Berger disposal.

In Europe, the latest actuarial assessments of the defined benefit schemes were at various dates between 1 January 1988 and 31 August 1988. The total market value of the assets at the valuation dates was £229 million (1989 £229 million). The combined actuarial value of the assets was 164% (1989 164%) of the combined value of accrued benefits, after allowing for expected future increases in earnings. These are no deficiencies on a current funding level basis.

In North America, the total market value of the assets of the major schemes at the last valuation dates was £6.4 million (1989 £5.8 million). The combined actuarial value of the assets was 89% (1989 97%) of the combined value of accrued benefits after allowing for expected future increases in earnings. There are no deficiencies on a current funding level basis. There are also post-retirement welfare benefit plans, which are expensed as benefits become payable. The £2.4 million (1989 £4.1 million) unfunded actuarial liability for these plans as at 31 December 1990 has been recognised in the group balance sheet as a deduction from debtors.

Exhibit 15.4 **Williams Holdings**

CONSOLIDATED BALANCE SHEET at 31 December 1990

	1990 £000	1989 £000
FIXED ASSETS		
Tangible assets	218,095	267,658
Investments	22,721	41
	240,816	267,699
CURRENT ASSETS		
Stocks	122,608	165,234
Debtors	**224,586**	273,361
Investments and other assets for sale	12,280	46,367
Cash	11,385	15,682
	370,859	500,644
CREDITORS: amounts falling due within one year		
Borrowings and finance leases	(10,115)	(71,836)
Other creditors	(254,022)	(300,597)
NET CURRENT ASSETS	106,722	128,211
TOTAL ASSETS LESS CURRENT LIABILITIES	347,538	395,910
CREDITORS: amounts falling due after more than one year		
Borrowings and finance leases	(5,897)	(106,875)
Other creditors	(997)	(1,816)
PROVISIONS FOR LIABILITIES AND CHARGES	(11,246)	(17,731)
	(18,140)	(126,422)
NET ASSETS	329,398	269,488
CAPITAL AND RESERVES		
Share capital	145,770	148,846
Reserves	183,628	120,642
TOTAL FUNDS	329,398	269,488

Williams Holdings showed a surplus of £72.8m in 1990 included within debtors of £225m. The inclusion of this surplus has the following effect on Williams' ratios:

Table 15.4   Williams Holdings

	As reported including surplus	Excluding pension surplus
Net Asset Value (£m)	329.4	256.6
Net Asset Value – per share (p)	106.6	83.0
Current Ratio	1.4	1.1
(Current Assets/Current Liabilities)		

Source: Williams Holdings Report and Accounts

Williams' capital gearing debt/equity calculation would also be affected by the inclusion of the pension fund prepayment asset, although this has not been shown as Williams was already lowly geared in 1990 so the effect was small. But even without the effect it is clear that the prepayment asset boosted stated Net Asset Value from 83p to 107p per share – a 28 per cent increase – and flattered the current ratio.

Why is this important to note? Referring back to earlier sections it is important to appreciate that a significant part of Williams' net assets and current assets is: 1) not realisable, unlike other assets, in that it cannot be turned into cash if needed by the company, 2) outside the control of management – it arises from a valuation by independent actuaries and 3) could disappear as readily as it appeared – a change in investment experience or assumptions for the fund, or in Williams' wage bill inflation could turn the surplus into a deficit at the next triennial valuation.

Whether a surplus can be controlled by a company's management is doubtful given the ability of outside agencies and legal changes to alter the position of the fund. Two examples are the Social Security Act 1990 and the Barber case. The Social Security Act introduced a mandatory requirement for indexation of pensions in payment by the annual increase in the Retail Price Index up to a maximum of five per cent p.a. The cost of implementing this requirement for past service could be as high as 50 per cent of disclosed pension fund liabilities, which would significantly erode surpluses. Obviously the cost for future service would not be as high.

The Barber judgement refers to a case before the European Court of Justice, which found that providing different pension benefits for men and women can be viewed as discriminatory. Most schemes have in the past provided for retirement by women at age 60 and men at age 65. It is not clear if this applies to past service rights (i.e. those already 'earned' by members) or future service only, but it was viewed seriously enough for a provision of £67m to be raised prior to the privatisation of National Power to cover the potential liability for past service:

Exhibit 15.5 **National Power and Powergen Main Prospectus**

Note 19. Pension arrangements

The Group participates in the industry-wide scheme, the Electricity Supply Pension Scheme, for the majority of its employees. This scheme is of the defined benefit type with assets invested in separate trustee administered funds.

In the six months ended 30 September 1990, the pension cost relating to the scheme amounted to £20 million and was assessed in accordance with the advice of a qualified actuary using the attained age method. An actuarial valuation of the scheme is carried out every three years by a qualified actuary, who recommends the rates of contribution payable by each group participating in the scheme. In intervening years the actuary reviews the continuing appropriateness of the rates. The latest actuarial assessment was at 31 March 1989. The assumptions which have the most significant effect on the results of the valuation are those relating to the rate of return on investments and the rates of increase in salaries and pensions. It was assumed that, over the long term, the annual rate of return on investments would be 2 per cent higher than the annual increase in salaries and 3.5 per cent higher than the annual increase in pensions.

At the date of the last actuarial valuation, the market value of the assets of the scheme that relate to the Group was £1,270 million and the actuarial value of those assets covered 101 per cent of the benefits that had accrued to members, after allowing for expected future increases in earnings.

In May 1990, the European Court of Justice decided that the practice of providing different pension benefits for men and women is discriminatory in certain circumstances. Whilst it is not yet certain whether the judgement applies to the past service rights of pension scheme members, a provision of £67 million was made at 31 March 1990 to reflect the probability of an additional past service liability arising.

There are also examples of other companies reacting to this judgement.

Exhibit 15.6 **The Boots Company Report and Accounts 1991**

22. PENSIONS

The group operates pension schemes throughout the world, most of which are final salary (defined benefit) schemes, and are fully funded.

The principal UK pension scheme is Boots Pension Scheme, the cost for which is determined by Bacon & Woodrow, consulting actuaries. The pension cost for Boots Pension Scheme was £8.7m for the period to 1 November 1989, from which date it was reduced to zero on the availability of the results of the 1 April 1989 valuation. The zero charge arises as a result of amortisation of surplus being recognised over 12 years, the expected average remaining service life of members, after benefit improvements. Recent benefit improvements to the scheme have anticipated the requirements of the Social Security Act 1990 regarding pension increases and the expected requirements for the equal provision for men and women following the judgement of the European Court of Justice in the case of Barber vs GRE Assurance Group. Allowance for these improvements was made in calculating the zero pension cost.

Given that both statute and case law are capable of affecting a company's pension fund liabilities, including case law from a supranational court, it seems that pension fund surpluses should not be ascribed quite the same certainty as some other assets.

But Williams is far from the most extreme example of the effect on a company's balance sheet from the creation of a prepayment asset representing a pension fund surplus.

Babcock's pension fund prepayment asset of £33.3m has the following affect on its ratios:

Table 15.5 Babcock International 1991

	As reported including surplus	Excluding pension surplus
Net Asset Value (£m)	70.2	36.9
Net Asset Value per share (p)	14.9	7.8
Current ratio	1.1	1.0

Of course, neither Williams' nor Babcock's share rating may be particularly dependent upon asset values – Babcock is primarily an engineering contractor, and contractors tend to fund their operations from prepayments and stage payments on contracts rather than from their own capital, but it is still worth noting that nearly half Babcock's asset value results from capitalisation of a pension fund surplus.

Exhibit 15.7 Babcock International Group Report and Accounts 1991

Note 14. DEBTORS

	Group 1991 £000	Group 1990 £000	Company 1991 £000	Company 1990 £000
Trade debtors	81,066	85,011	-	-
Amounts recoverable on contracts	48,580	32,873	-	-
Amounts owed by subsidiary undertakings	-	-	1,873	2,000
Amounts owed by associated undertakings	105	166	-	-
Prepayments and accrued income	3,218	1,062	-	-
Pension fund surpluses	**33,266**	**34,366**	-	-
Other debtors	12,035	10,019	7,479	213
	178,270	163,497	9,352	2,213

Included in debtors are the following amounts which are due after more than one year:

	Group 1991 £000	Group 1990 £000	Company 1991 £000	Company 1990 £000
Trade debtors	7,832	6,392	-	-
Pension fund surpluses	**31,366**	**33,366**	-	-
Other debtors	2,951	98	2,828	-
	42,149	39,856	2,828	-

Note 20. PENSION FUNDING

The group operates a number of different pension arrangements throughout the world, according to local requirements of each country. The total pension costs of the group were as follows:

18 July 1989 to 31 March 1990 £000		Year to 31 March 1991 £000	Year to 31 March 1990 £000
8,432	UK schemes	12,336	11,428
410	Overseas schemes	1,877	710
8,842		14,212	12,138

The three major schemes, which cover 56% of all group employees, are in the UK and South Africa and are of the defined benefit type. In each case the scheme is funded by payments to separate trustee administered funds and the pension cost is assessed in accordance with the advice of independent, qualified actuaries. The details of the latest valuation of these schemes are as follows:

	UK schemes Babcock Thorn	UK schemes Babcock Group	South Africa
Number of employees	5,023	2,850	755
Date of last valuation	31.3.90	31.3.89	31.3.91
Method of valuation	Attained age	Projected unit	Projected unit
Results of last valuation:			
- market value of assets	£113 million	£279 million	£22 million
- level of funding	100%	113%	125%
Principal valuation assumptions:			
- excess of investment returns over earnings increases	1.50%	2.00%	1.00%
- excess of investment returns over pension increases	3.00%-6.00%	6.00%	5.00%
- annual rate of dividend growth	4.50%	4.25%	4.25%

The surpluses in the Babcock Group UK scheme and the South African scheme are carried as a prepayment in the balance sheet at £33.3 million (1990 £34.3 million), and are being corrected in the short term by a suspension of the group's contributions. An actuarial review of the Babcock Group UK scheme, since the last valuation, has reported investment performance which is significantly in excess of that assumed and recent legislation which is likely to lead to increased pension costs in future years, although neither of these can yet be quantified precisely.

Exhibit 15.8   **Babcock International Group Balance Sheet at 31 March 1991**

	£000	1991 £000	£000	1990 £000
Fixed assets				
Tangible assets		89,942		63,040
Investments		5,245		6,342
		95,187		69,382
Current assets				
Stocks	39,684		40,715	
Debtors	178,270		163,497	
Cash and bank balances	92,609		87,286	
	310,563		291,498	
Creditors:				
Amounts falling due within one year	(274,072)		(248,386)	
Net current assets		36,491		43,112
Total assets less current liabilities				
Creditors:				
Amounts falling due after more than one year		(19,363)		(14,435)
Provisions for liabilities and charges		(42,096)		(32,168)
Net Assets		70,219		65,891
Capital and reserves				
Called up share capital		47,130		47,130
Share premium account		10,962		10,962
Profit and loss account		7,954		4,831
		66,046		62,923
Minority interests		4,173		2,968
		70,219		65,891

Certain corresponding amounts in respect of the previous period within the categories of stocks, debtors and creditors have been restated to present better the group's long-term contract-related balances.

OTHER PROBLEMS WITH SSAP 24

1) Interest and Investment Income

When an asset arises in a company's balance sheet because the pension fund cost charged in the profit and loss account differs from the regular cost, SSAP 24 permits notional interest earned on this asset to be credited to the profit and loss account. In the case of Ratners, net interest on the surplus of £1.5m was accrued in determining the annual pension cost of £922,000:

Exhibit 15.9 Ratners Annual Report and Accounts 1991

Note 6. PROFIT ON ORDINARY ACTIVITIES BEFORE TAXATION

	1991 £000	1990 £000
Profit on ordinary activities before taxation is stated after charging:		
Share incentive scheme	250	500
Depreciation and amortisation	29,127	22,209
Depreciation on finance lease assets	-	79
Pension costs	**922**	**663**
Auditor's remuneration	418	371
Operating lease rentals:		
Plant and machinery	88	145
Property	80,945	63,554

Note 14. DEBTORS

	1991 Group £000	1991 Company £000	1990 Group £000
Trade debtors	74,006	13,616	38,165
Amounts owed by subsidiary companies	-	63,599	-
Other debtors	11,546	3,084	11,368
Corporation tax recoverable	22,645	6,685	3,349
Prepayments and accrued income	16,125	5,853	10,244
Debtors due within one year	124,322	92,837	63,236
Pension fund prepayment	**16,702**	-	17,012
	141,024	92,837	80,248

Note 23. PENSION FUND COSTS

The Group operates a number of pension schemes in the UK. The majority of the schemes are of the defined benefit type. The assets of the schemes are held in separate trustee administered funds. Contributions to the schemes, which are assessed in accordance with the advice of an independent qualified actuary using the projected unit method of valuation, are charged to the profit and loss account so as to spread the cost of pensions over employees' working lives with the Group.

The most recent actuarial valuation of the main scheme, the H Samuel group pension scheme, was at 6 April 1988. The principal actuarial assumptions adopted in the valuation were that, over the long term, the investment rate of return would be 9% per annum, and this would exceed future pensionable earnings increases by 1.5% per annum and increases to present and future pensions in payment by 4% per annum. It was also assumed that dividend increases on the equity portfolio would average 4.5% per annum. The actuarial value of the assets was sufficient to cover 148% of the benefits that had accrued to members at the valuation date, after allowing for expected future increases in earnings and pensions. The market value of the scheme's assets at 6 April 1988 was £49.6 million.

The surplus relating to the Group's UK pension arrangements at 2 February 1991 of £16,702,000 has been reflected in the balance sheet. The movement in the surplus of £310,000 is stated in the net interest of £1,456,000 accrued during the year on the prepayment, and is included in the Group charge of £922,000 in note 6.

This is intended to reflect the return which this prepayment asset is earning as part of the pension fund. Once again, this represents the investment return which is building up on that part of the pension fund representing the surplus – but it is not interest or investment income available in cash to the company.

A practice which can also lead to potentially misleading financial ratios is crediting the surplus when it is spread over the average life of scheme members against interest payable since this can produce a potentially dangerous misconception about the level of interest cover:

Exhibit 15.10 **Courtaulds Textiles Report and Accounts 1990**

Note 2. INTEREST PAYABLE NET OF INTEREST INCOME	1990	1989
	£m	£m
Interest element of finance lease payments	0.9	1.0
Interest on bank and other borrowings fully repayable within five years	17.1	15.9
Interest payable on long-term borrowings	0.4	0.7
Interest payable	18.4	17.6
Interest receivable	(6.6)	(5.2)
	11.8	12.4

The interest charges for 1989 are proforma, details are provided in note 22

Note 20. PENSION COMMITMENTS

The Group participates in a number of pension schemes around the world. The major schemes are of the defined benefit type with assets held in separate trustee administered funds.

Before demerger from Courtaulds plc, Courtaulds Textiles participated in the Courtaulds plc UK Pension Scheme. This scheme was reviewed by consulting actuaries, as at 31 March 1990, using the projected unit method, to determine the proportion of the Fund to be transferred to the Courtaulds Textiles Pension Scheme. The principal actuarial assumptions were that over the long term, the annual rate of return in investments would be 1.5% higher than the annual increase in total pensionable remuneration and 4.5% higher than the annual increase in present and future pension payments. The actuarial value of the assets was sufficient to cover 169% of the benefits which had accrued to members, after allowing for benefit improvements announced in 1989 and expected future increases in pensionable remuneration. On the recommendation of the actuaries no company contributions have been made to the scheme since 1 January 1990 and this will continue for a period of five years, subject to the next actuarial valuation expected to be as at 31 March 1992. SSAP 24 requires the Fund to be valued on a reasonable best estimate basis rather than with the very prudent assumptions used by the Trustees in funding the Scheme, which are referred to above. In accounting for pension costs under SSAP 24, the principal actuarial assumptions were that the rate of

---

Exhibit 15.10 (contd.) **Courtaulds Textiles Report and Accounts 1990**

return on investments would be 2% higher than the annual increase in total pensionable remuneration and 5% higher than the increase in pensions. On this basis the Fund of the new Courtaulds Textiles Pension Scheme was calculated to have an excess of assets over liabilities of £95m and the actuarial value of the assets was sufficient to cover 193% of the benefits which had accrued to members. The market value of the assets at 31 March 1990 was £171.3m. The surplus is being spread over the 11 year average remaining service lives of the current UK employees. The effect of this is a net pension credit to profit before taxation in 1990 of £4.4m (1989 £3.0m) which represents the benefit, in excess of the regular pension cost, arising from the pension fund surplus. **In 1990 this credit has reduced interest payable by £4.4m (1989 £4.0m)** with a nil (1989 £1.0m) charge to operating profit. As noted above, no company contributions have been paid since 1 January 1990; during 1989 the Company paid pension contributions of £5.0m. The effect of introducing SSAP 24 in 1989 was a benefit of £8.0m.

The actuarial value of the assets of pension schemes abroad approximates to the benefits which have accrued to members, after allowing for expected future increases in pensionable remuneration.

Note 2. Interest payable net of investment income	*1991*	*1990*
	£m	*£m*
Interest element of finance lease payments	3.2	3.0
Interest on bank and other borrowings fully repayable		
within five years	39.2	51.8
Interest payable on long-term borrowings	1.7	5.7
Interest payable	44.1	60.5
Other interest receivable	(39.2)	(52.5)
	4.9	8.0

Note 27. Pensions commitments

In accounting for pension costs under SSAP 24, the rate of return on investments has been assumed to be 2% higher than the increase in pensionable remuneration and 5% higher in pensions. On this basis the actuarial value of the assets was sufficient to cover 138% of the benefits that have accrued to members after allowing for benefit improvements announced in 1989 and expected future increases in pensionable remuneration. The share of this actuarial surplus is being spread over the 12 years average remaining service life of current Courtaulds employees.

The actuarial value of the assets of pension schemes abroad approximated to the benefits that had accrued to members, after allowing for expected future increases in pensionable remuneration. The Group's US subsidiary undertakings have no significant health and medical plans providing post-retirement benefits.

The pension credit arising from the application of SSAP 24 increased operating profit by £4.3m (1990 £13.8m) and reduced interest payable net of investment income by £14.4m (1990 £15.5m). A prepayment of £42.0m (1990 £23.3m) is included in debtors representing the excess of the pension credit to the profit and loss account over the amounts funded and excludes credits transferred to Courtaulds Textiles.

Table 15.6 Effect on interest cover

	Year to 31 December 1990 Courtaulds	Courtaulds Textiles
Reported		
Operating profit	187.4	51.7
Net interest payable	(4.9)	(11.8)
Interest cover (times)	38.2	4.4
less Pension Fund credit		
Net interest payable less pension credit	(19.3)	(16.2)
Revised interest cover	9.7	3.2

In neither case could the Courtauld companies interest cover slip to a dangerous level if the pension fund credit is deducted. But it is as well to perform the calculation – bankers are only interested in whether their interest charge is covered by actual cash received, and an amortised pension fund surplus certainly does not fall into this category. In the case of Courtaulds plc the interest earned by the fund surplus has been included in interest income.

ASB DISCUSSION PAPER

A discussion paper on Pension costs was issued by the ASB in June 1995. It attempts to solve some of the most glaring problems involved in interpreting companies' pension fund accounting by standardisation and disclosure in accounts.

Standardisation applies to the actuarial approach and in the method of spreading a surplus or deficit. At present under SSAP 24, disclosure is so poor that if two companies had identical surpluses to those used as an example in Table 15.2, since they do not have to disclose the method used for spreading the surplus, the impact on the first year's profit & loss account could still vary by 50%. The discussion paper plumps for the straight line method as the proposed standard method for spreading a surplus. This has the disadvantage that it tends to 'up front' the benefit of the surplus, but at least standardisation has the result of levelling the playing field, so that one company's results including the benefit of a pension surplus will be able to be compared more readily with another.

Disclosure of the actuarial assumptions which have produced the surplus should also be improved.

This is to be welcomed since SSAP 24 is in my view one of the least comprehensible Standards, with items such as amortising a surplus which can be so large that the annual amortised amount is bigger than the company's regular contribution and leads to a negative charge to the profit & loss account – whatever that means, since no money passes hands from the pension fund to the company. Or the fact that interest on the surplus remaining on the pension fund each year is credited to the profit & loss account although no cash passes from the fund to the company. Anything which makes pension fund accounting and SSAP 24 in particular more comprehensible is welcome, but this does not improve the 'quality' of this item in accounts.

The fact is that a pension fund surplus is still a) the result of an actuary's guess, b) does not necessarily represent any cash benefit, and c) the whole point of SSAP 24 is to make it disappear by amortising it over the years. Investors would therefore do well to apply a large dose of scepticism to this element of profits or any related prepayment asset in the balance sheet, rather than worrying too much about the intricacies of pension fund accounting methods.

16

GOODWILL

An attitude of kindness, friendliness or benevolence
Oxford English Dictionary

Goodwill is the accounting term given to the difference between the price paid for an acquisition and the fair value of the assets acquired. It has been an increasing feature of UK and other countries' take-overs as the main industries have turned away from manufacturing and other asset based activities, and towards service industries, consumer brand management and so-called people businesses which have few fixed assets if indeed they have any. Apart from the premium to asset values often paid for control in take-overs, the growth of businesses whose performance is not based upon assets has also inflated the amount of goodwill involved in take-overs.

Another factor which has increased the amount of goodwill in take-overs is the use of pre-acquisition write-downs of the sort covered in Chapter 4. The Coloroll acquisition of John Crowther used as an example in the first edition of this book is a classic example:

Exhibit 16.1 **Coloroll Group Accounts for the year ended 31st March 1989**

18. Reserves

	Share premium account £000	Revaluation reserve £000	Other reserves £000	Profit and loss account £000	Total £000
(a) Group					
At 1st April, 1988	24,929	-	15,733	25,119	65,781
Premium on shares issued for cash	22,623	-	-	-	22,623
Premium on shares issued on acquisition of subsidiaries	-	-	183,681	-	183,681
Purchase of Coloroll Finance Limited stock (note 17)	-	-	158	-	158
* **Goodwill written off**	-	-	**(247,257)**	-	**(247,257)**
Retained profit for the year	-	0	0	26,879	26,879
Exchange differences	-	-	-	166	166
Property revaluation	-	8,711	-	-	8,711
At 31st March, 1989	47,552	8,711	(47,685)	52,164	60,742

Coloroll had paid a premium of £145m to Crowther's stated net asset value which would have constituted the goodwill in Coloroll's balance sheet. However, Coloroll's fair value accounting led to a further £75m in write-downs and reorganisation provisions. The result was that an acquisition which cost £215m produced goodwill of £224m. Why is this significant? Because returns matter.

GROWTH VERSUS RATE OF RETURN

As the quote from Ian Hay Davison on pages 51 indicates, the single statistic which commands more attention than any other in investment is earnings per share, and in particular growth in earnings per share. The simple assumption of techniques for valuing shares using growth in EPS is that the higher the sustainable growth rate in EPS for a company, the higher the Price/Earnings multiple should be. But growth is only one part of the valuation process.

Take a simple example. If you were looking for somewhere to invest some cash you might decide to visit some building societies to find the best deal. If you asked three societies, called originally enough societies A, B and C, for their best deal for an investment of £10,000 and they offered a rate which grew at A-10%, B-15% and C-20% p.a. which one would you choose?

If the answer you would give is the one which is guaranteed to grow at 20% p.a. then you are making the same mistake as investors who concentrate upon growth in EPS as their sole measure of company performance. What if the same societies' initial rate which is going to grow is A-5%, B-3% and C-1% p.a., respectively? Clearly this would alter your choice since the first society is offering an initial rate of return five times greater than that of society C. In year two, the rates would increase to A-5.05%, B-3.45% and C-1.2%. Which society you choose to invest in is a more complex choice than simply selecting the one with the highest growth rate. It would depend upon how long you expected each one to grow the rate offered and something called the time value of money. The rate offered by B will grow to over 5% in four years, but apart from the fact that A's rate will also have grown by then, albeit at a slower rate, there is also the fact that A has been delivering a higher return during the intervening years. This idea of the time value of money is the concept behind Discounted Cash Flow.

What you are discovering here is that it is not only the rate at which an investment's return grows which is important but also the initial rate of return. How do we measure this rate of return for companies? Typically by calculating their return on capital or return on equity by dividing profits by equity or total capital and expressing this as a percentage.

The UK GAAP treatment of goodwill introduces a problem in achieving this, since the UK is the only major accounting regime in the world which allows companies to write off goodwill incurred against reserves in the balance sheet.

Table 16.1 **INTERNATIONAL PRACTICE - GOODWILL**

- US & Canada : Amortise through Profit & Loss A/C
  - max 40 yrs
- Australia : Amortise through Profit & Loss A/C
  - max 20 yrs
- Germany : Amortise through Profit & Loss A/C
  - short period
- UK : Immediate write off to reserves

Why is this a problem? There are even some analysts who maintain that it is 'conservative' to write goodwill off immediately. But the return calculation which you need to perform in order to determine what return a company is delivering uses those reserves as part of the denominator in the calculation:

$$\text{Rate of Return} = \frac{\text{Profits}}{\text{Capital}}$$

where capital includes share capital plus reserves, and sometimes debt capital as well.

There is more than one way to make this return measure look good. One would be to inflate profits, and many techniques of creative accounting are aimed squarely at this. But just as good is decreasing the denominator or capital base and that is exactly what happens when goodwill is written off. And what a happy coincidence: when a company makes pre-acquisition write-downs it both depresses the capital base by increasing the goodwill write-off, and increases future profits as reorganisation provisions are utilised and assets written down are realised.

This is why in order to get a realistic picture of the return which a company is delivering it is necessary to add back to the capital base the cumulative goodwill written off.

THE CARLTON COMMUNICATIONS EXAMPLE

Carlton Communications has been an acquisitive company in recent years. It bought Technicolor which gave rise to goodwill of over £500m.

Goodwill of almost £500m was also written off on the acquisition of UEI. The Pickwick acquisition added another £100m to goodwill, and a further £671m came from the acquisition of Central Television. The result is that Carlton had total goodwill written off of over £1.5bn by 1995. To be fair, Carlton discloses this figure in a very up front manner on the face of the balance sheet.

Exhibit 16.2 **Carlton Communications 1995 Annual Report**

Consolidated balance sheet
30 September 1995

	Notes	£m	1995 £m	£m	1994 £m
Attributable to:					
Equity shareholders' funds (before goodwill)			**1,588.6**		1,464.2
Cumulative goodwill written off directly to reserves			**(1,528.6)**		(1,538.5)
Equity shareholders' funds			**60.0**		(74.3)
Non-equity shareholders' funds	25		**407.3**		414.8
Total shareholders' funds			**467.3**		340.5

Although Carlton is very open about its goodwill written off, many other companies only include this figure in the notes to the accounts. But it is of no use, even if the disclosure of an accounting item is exemplary, if analysts and investors do not think about the implications of the figures disclosed.

Basically Carlton has expended the money represented by this goodwill on shareholders' behalf, so what sort of return have they earned on it?

Table 16.2 **Carlton Communications**

Return on Equity including and excluding goodwill

Year to 30th September	1994 £m	1995 £m
Attributable profit after tax		165.2
Shareholders' funds	340.5	467.3
Average shareholders' funds		403.9
Return on average equity		**40.9%**
Goodwill	1538.5	1528.6
Average shareholders' funds plus goodwill		1937.5
Return on average equity plus goodwill		**8.5%**

The table shows that Carlton has managed to generate an apparently spectacular 40%+ return on average equity in 1995 (average is used to give a fairer measure since the level of equity changes during the year). But if goodwill written off is added back, Carlton's ROE drops to a more pedestrian 8%. In 1995 it was close to the long gilt yield, so that Carlton was not providing any excess return over the gilt rate to compensate for the risk inherent in shares.

Of course it is possible that Carlton's returns are about to accelerate so rapidly that it is worth accepting these returns at the outset as investors often do with a high growth stock in technology or biotech. Arguments may also rage about the true nature of the goodwill incurred. For example, when Carlton bid for Central Television, the share price of both companies rose so that Carlton paid an even greater premium over Central's net assets than it had originally envisaged. However, the point remains that investors would massively overestimate Carlton's returns, as with any acquisitive company, unless some adjustment is made for goodwill, and returns are important.

Other methods of assessing performance used by investors that focus solely upon growth may be misleading when a company is expanding as rapidly as Carlton has:

Table 16.3 **Carlton Communications**

EPS Growth

	1991	1992	1993	1994	1995	Compound Growth p.a.
EPS (p)	25.4	33.4	42.0	53.8	65.3	20.8%

Carlton's earnings per share have indeed grown by a compound rate of over 20% p.a. over the past five years, but at the same time the rate of return on capital has been depressed by the ever greater quantities of equity which have been issued to fund the acquisitions behind this growth. An investor who bought Carlton's shares purely because of the growth would be in danger of making the same mistake as the depositor who chose building society C in the illustrative example above.

It gives some clue to what is really happening when a company is required to report its results under US GAAP because like Carlton it has American Depositary Receipts (ADR's) or some other securities registered with the US Securities and Exchange Commission.

Exhibit 16.3 **Carlton Communications US GAAP Results**

Approximate cumulative effect on shareholders' equity of differences between UK and US GAAP

	1995 US$m*	1994 US$m*
Shareholders' equity per UK GAAP	739.7	539.1
Approximate cumulative effect of differences between UK GAAP and US GAAP	2,116.4	2,177.0
Approximate shareholders' equity as adjusted for US GAAP	**2,856.1**	**2,716.1**
Attributable to:		
Ordinary shareholders	2,211.4	2,059.4
Preference shareholders	644.7	656.7
	2,856.1	2,716.1
Approximate effect on net income of differences between UK and US GAAP		
Income for the financial year attributable to holders of Ordinary shares, per UK GAAP	238.2	185.2
Approximate effect on net income of differences between UK GAAP and US GAAP	105.6	77.5
Approximate net income attributable to holders of Ordinary shares under US GAAP	132.6	107.7

US accounting regulations are far more prescriptive than the UK equivalent, allowing far less discretion over how items are treated. They also have some key differences such as the requirement to capitalise goodwill on the balance sheet and amortise it by an annual charge to the profit & loss account. The result of this and other adjustments for Carlton is that translating its 1995 results into US GAAP increased shareholders' equity to $2856m and reduced net profit to $132.6m: a return of just 4.6%. Given this tougher accounting regime it is easy to see why US companies find it harder than their UK counterparts to get away with vague statements about the absence of dilution from acquisitions.

Investors should always look to see if the company they are contemplating investing in is required to report under US GAAP, and if so take notice of the figures. If not, they should still calculate the return on equity or the pre interest return on all forms of capital including debt. Is this return adequate? Is it significantly above the risk free rate of return represented by the long gilt yield for example? If not, is the company about to grow its profits so rapidly without requiring an equivalent amount of additional capital (a vital point this!) that its returns will soon rise to more than compensate for their initial paucity? Comparisons should also be made with peer group returns generated by other companies in the same industry, and sophisticated investors might like to compare the company's returns with some estimate of its cost of capital.

These simple calculations turn the reported returns on capital which some acquisitive companies are delivering from the spectacular into something which is more pedestrian:

Table 16.4 Adjusting for goodwill (1990/91)

	% *Published*	*ROE*	% *Adjusted*
BET	27		4.0
Boots	18		9
Bowater	18		10
Carlton Comms	15		4.5
Grand Metropolitan	18		10
Harrison & Crosfield	9		5.7
RHM	18		6.4
Reed	12		7.9
Pearson	14		8.5
TI	27		10

Table 16.4 shows the return on equity delivered by some of the UK's most acquisitive companies calculated a) Published – on the basis of stated capital, and b) Adjusted – with cumulative goodwill previously written off added back. It is easy to see why anyone judging these companies on their stated returns on capital could have made a grave error which could have led them to lose money: the actual returns on capital were poor once the goodwill paid for acquisitions was added back.

Of course, amongst the most acquisitive companies are the UK's conglomerates, which are now classified by the FT-Actuaries as part of the Diversified Industrials sector. They have had to be major exponents of goodwill accounting given the number of acquisitions they have undertaken, and their use of pre-acquisition write downs and reorganisation provisions in particular. The result of adding back goodwill in calculating their returns over the past six years is shown in Table 16.5.

Table 16.5 Return on Invested Capital (including goodwill added back)

Year ending	1989	1990	1991	1992	1993	1994
FTSE						
BTR	24.8%	22.6%	15.1%	15.6%	15.5%	n.a.
Hanson	11.7%	12.2%	9.1%	8.6%	6.1%	7.0%
Tomkins	n.a.	10.0%	12.9%	14.0%	10.4%	11.4%
Williams	15.7%	12.1%	13.5%	10.4%	11.3%	n.a.
Gen Industrials UK-ROCE*	**19.8%**	**19.0%**	**15.5%**	**11.5%**	**11.8%**	

ROIC nos. are averaged using both opening and closing capital amounts where possible
* The Gen. Industrials ROCE is sourced from Datastream, and while it does not add back goodwill, this item is likely to be almost negligible when taken across the market as a whole.

The conglomerates have underperformed the average industrial company in return on capital in every year shown in the table. This is a rather startling result. Conglomerates have to pay a premium above the market price when they take over a company, but the aim of conglomerates is to more than compensate for the handicap which this premium represents by superior management of the businesses acquired. Clearly this has not been achieved by the UK's major conglomerates in recent years, and for once the stock market seems now to have factored this into the sector's share price performance:

Figure 16.1 Diversified Industrials relative to the FT All Share Index

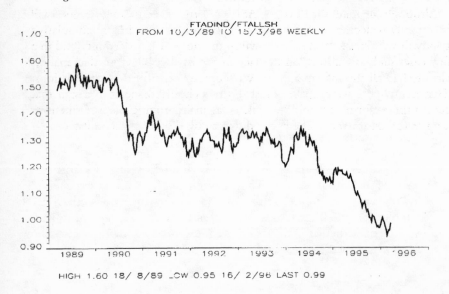

HIGH 1.60 18/ 8/89 LOW 0.95 16/ 2/96 LAST 0.99

ASB WORKING PAPER

An ASB working paper on Goodwill and intangible assets was issued in June 1995 based upon a discussion paper issued in 1993. It proposes that the UK should move closer to international practice by retaining goodwill as an intangible asset on the balance sheet. There is then a presumption that goodwill has a finite life of twenty years or less and should therefore be amortised through the profit and loss account over this period. But if the life of goodwill cannot be readily determined, it can remain on the balance sheet but instead of being reduced by an annual amortisation charge it is subject to an annual review in order to determine whether the value of the goodwill has been permanently impaired and therefore needs to be written down.

The proposed method of reviewing goodwill is to compare the value of the acquisition in the balance sheet (net assets plus goodwill) with the discounted net present value of future earnings streams. This sounds very sophisticated, but I suspect that the impairment review is a cop-out when most other countries require amortisation of goodwill through the profit & loss account. It will be interesting to see whether the impairment review produces any more write downs of goodwill than the reviews of the value of brands on the balance sheet have done over the years.

However, despite some dissatisfaction with this element of the ASB's proposals, it is frankly not that important. What is of greater significance is the fact that goodwill will at least remain on the balance sheet to remind investors that these sums of money have been expended by the company on their behalf, and should therefore be included in the capital base on which the company is expected to earn a return.

Although the main thrust of the ASB's reform of accounting for goodwill is certainly welcome, it should also have been irrelevant in that cumulative goodwill written off is already shown in the notes to the accounts, and in a few cases such as Carlton, on the face of the balance sheet, so that analysts already had all the information they needed to perform these calculations. That many or more probably most did not choose to do so is a sign that accounting reform can only take us so far in improving the assessment of corporate performance. The rest is down to us as users of accounts.

17

DEFERRED TAX

Hope deferred maketh the heart sick
Proverbs 13:12

Few subjects can seem more arcane than deferred taxation. Just reading the 'Explanatory note' at the start of the Standard which currently governs the treatment of deferred tax in the UK makes this clear. The opening sentence is: "This statement is concerned with accounting for tax on profits and surpluses which are recognised in the financial statements in one period but assessed in another." Quite!

Deferred tax is currently governed by SSAP 15 which was first issued in 1978. The amount of tax which a UK company has to pay in respect of a particular accounting period can sometimes bear little or no relationship to reported profits. In general this is because companies' tax liabilities are assessed on a different basis to their statutory accounts. In particular, some items of income are tax free, so although they may create a profit it is non-taxable. Conversely, some expense items are not tax allowable deductions. These items create permanent differences between companies' reported profits and taxable profits. In other cases there are items which are included in companies' accounts for a different period to that in which they are dealt with for taxation purposes. These create so-called timing differences, and it is these that raise the problem of deferred taxation.

TIMING DIFFERENCES

The best and simplest example of a timing difference can occur when a company purchases a fixed asset.

Table 17.1   £100 Fixed asset purchase

Year	1	2	3	4	5	6	7
Depreciation	10	10	10	10	10	10	10
Writing down tax allowance of 25%	25	18.8	14.1	10.6	7.9	6.0	4.5
Excess tax allowance	15	8.8	4.1	0.6	(2.1)	(4.0)	(5.5)

Take the example shown in the table of a company which purchases a fixed asset for £100 and decides to depreciate it in a straight line over ten years. Its profit and loss account will bear a charge of £10 p.a. However, the tax treatment of fixed asset purchases is for the company to receive a writing down allowance so that a part of the cost of the asset is allowed against profits each year. The table shows the effect of a writing down allowance of 25% p.a. In the first year, for example, tax is calculated by adding back the depreciation charge of £10 since depreciation is not a tax allowable deduction, otherwise the company would be given tax relief twice: once through depreciation and then again through the writing down allowance. Then the writing down allowance of £25 is deducted and tax is calculated on the new taxable profit figure which is £15 lower than the reported figure since £10-£25=-£15.

This situation will continue for some years as long as 25% of the residual value of the asset is greater than the £10 depreciation charge. But it is inevitable that the situation will reverse because both the tax and the depreciation charge are only writing off the £100 cost of the asset. As a result, in Year 5 the depreciation charge exceeds the tax allowance for the first time, and if this were the only influence, taxable profits would as a result be higher than reported profits.

What's all this got to do with deferred tax? By the end of Year 4 this company will have postponed payment of tax which will become payable over the next few years. How should it account for this? Should it show the full amount of tax payable on its profits from Year 1 as if the accelerated capital allowances did not exist? Or should it just ignore the problem and report a much lower amount of tax in the early years when the writing down allowance being greater than depreciation cuts its tax bill? After all, one thing seems likely to come to its rescue: few companies purchase a single fixed asset, so won't the accelerated writing down allowances on later asset purchases cause the same effect to be repeated?

SSAP 15 allows the company to follow what is called the partial provision basis in accounting for deferred tax: just accounting for tax which is deferred by, say, capital allowances only to the extent that it expects it to become payable in the foreseeable future.

TREES DON'T GROW TO THE SKY

The example is unrealistic because virtually no company ever has a single transaction in which it purchases a single fixed asset. Companies are continually purchasing assets. True, and as a result SSAP 15 gives companies discretion over whether they should account for the tax that may become payable when the excess of capital allowances over depreciation begins to reverse. This is based upon an assessment of whether the tax liabilities which can be deferred by capital allowances will actually fall due and payable in the foreseeable future. This in turn depends upon future levels of profit and tax allowances, which will be influenced amongst other things by future capital expenditure plans.

So what's the problem? Companies are notoriously bad at predicting some of the items which need to be assessed in order to make a decision on whether it is necessary to make full provision for deferred tax. Take the case of a company which is expanding rapidly. It is purchasing more and more fixed assets. As a result its capital allowances continually outweigh its depreciation charge. Under the partial provision method allowed by SSAP 15 it may reach the conclusion that this is a situation which seems likely to continue. But it may miss one important factor in reaching this conclusion: there is a recession coming. When the recession hits, the company's profits and cash flow fall. As a result, it decides to drop its capital expenditure programme. The result of this is that the excess of capital allowances over depreciation begins to reverse and the tax charge rises. In effect what happens is that the Revenue wants to collect the tax which would have been due in respect of earlier years had it not been for the capital allowances. Needless to say, it can be a dangerous situation for a company to have to drop its capital expenditure programme because it is short of cash, only to find itself presented with a tax demand it had not expected.

If you think these circumstances are extreme, think about this. Isn't it inevitable that eventually all companies will reduce their capital expenditure plans? Otherwise they would become bigger than the economy they operate in. Moreover, it is obvious that what is needed to stave off tax bills by means of capital allowances on new fixed assets is not just continuing capital expenditure, but continually accelerating capital expenditure, something which companies are even more unlikely to be able to deliver.

Moreover, if a company's tax charge rises unexpectedly it will obviously have a damaging effect upon earnings per share and so upon the share price. The damage can be even greater than simply the effect of falling earnings.

THE BANKS SECTOR EXAMPLE

The publication of SSAP 15 on Deferred Tax coincided with a Corporation Tax regime in the UK which gave 100% first year capital allowances on capital expenditure together with a recession which robbed most of corporate UK of its taxable profits. Companies therefore had substantial tax allowances from their capital expenditure but no profits against which to set them.

The banks came to the rescue. The recession of 1979–81 saw high interest rates as the Thatcher government tried to extinguish inflation. The clearing banks still enjoyed a substantial interest free current account base at this time, so that the higher rates made them very profitable. So profitable in fact that the government imposed a 'once for all' bank tax in 1981 to remove some of these 'windfall' profits. The solution to the commercial and industrial companies tax allowances was for the banks to purchase the capital equipment and to lease it to the corporate sector. The banks obtained the benefit of the 100% first year allowances and passed on some of this to the lessees in the form of lower lease rentals.

Everyone was happy, except perhaps the Chancellor of the Exchequer who could see the banks with substantial profits sheltering them behind the capital allowances system. The banks meanwhile were accounting for this tax which was deferred by 100% first year allowances by the partial provision method. In the main they appeared to believe that this regime of 100% first allowances and an ever rising level of demand in the form of industrial capital expenditure would go on for the foreseeable future, and made no provision for deferred tax which was in line with SSAP 15. The tax deferred by this method therefore became part of the banks' reserves as it boosted retained profits.

Figure 17.1   The Banks sector relative to the All Share Index after the 1984 Budget

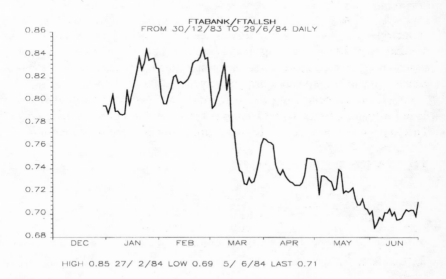

FTABANK/FTALLSH
FROM 30/12/83 TO 29/6/84 DAILY

HIGH 0.85 27/ 2/84 LOW 0.69   5/ 6/84 LAST 0.71

Disaster struck in 1984 when the Budget removed 100% first year allowances and replaced them with 25% annual writing down allowances. At a stroke the government had crystallised much of the previously unprovided deferred tax since with allowances reduced from 100% to 25% in the first year, the banks would have needed to quadruple their purchases of equipment just to stand still. Large amounts of what had been regarded as the banks' capital was effectively switched into deferred tax overnight, leaving the sector short of capital and triggering a series of rights issues. The effect on share prices was devastating, as shown in Figure 17.1.

Clearly both the banks and the market had been wrong in their assessment of whether the deferred tax would become payable, and investors lost money in consequence.

ACCOUNTING FOR TAX

The ASB intends to remedy this reliance upon corporate guesswork in assessing the need to provide for deferred tax. The discussion paper 'Accounting for tax' published in March 1995 suggested a move away from partial provisioning to the full provisioning method in line with US GAAP. If this was accepted, companies would need to provide for the whole of the annual tax liability ignoring any ability to defer part of it and timing differences, so reporting a conservative tax charge.

However, the uproar from companies faced with the possibility of a sharp rise in their tax charge was deafening, and it is possible the ASB will backtrack and limit its reforms to some tightening of the partial provision rules. That companies should attempt to head off a move to the full provision method is understandable. This method is likely to lead to some overstatement of tax liabilities over time, and the effect on some companies' reported earnings could be significant. The following table shows those large companies which might show a significant fall in EPS with a move to full provisioning based upon their 1993 accounts:

Table 17.2   Large companies where full provision for deferred tax could produce
>10% fall in earnings

Company	Estimated EPS fall %	Company figures or Est.	Capex up/down + -	Comments (references are to 1993/4 annual report)
Arjo Wiggins	14.8	E	?	Capex up in '93 but commitments down in Note 23, page 32
BAA	11.8	C	+	£1.4bn capex planned over three years vs. £320m in year to 3/94.
British Airways	36.4	C	–	Capex fell in 93/4 from £577m to £320m (page 44). No new aircraft orders placed (page 10) see extract attached
British Gas	20.5★	C	–	Capex fell from £2bn to £1.6bn in '93
BP	11.7★★	C	–	Overshadowed by forecast 100% recovery in EPS in '94
Cable & Wireless	16.5	C	–	Capex if £1.3bn planned over 3 years vs. £1bn in year to 3/94 (page 31)
GKN	12.4	C	–	Commitments in note 26, page 61 of annual accounts
NFC	21.6	E	–	Note 26, page 62
Northern Electric	11.7	C	+	Page 16, and capex authorised up (Note 25, page 40)
Scottish Hydro	10.7	X	–	Note 23, page 24
Severn Trent	25.3	C	–	Page 1, capex authorised down (Note 19, page 35)
Southern Electric	12.9	E	?	Up in 93/4 (page 9) but commitments down (Note 27, page 38)
Thames Water	30.2	E	?	Note 29, page 46. Down in 93/4 followed completion of London Ring Main
TI Group	13.8	C	–	Capex authorised down in Note 28, page 54. Capex down in '93 esp at Dowty (page 22)

Notes
★ Based on CCA earnings of 15.1p per share in '93 adjusted to exclude restructuring costs
★★ Based upon LIFO Net Income of £1125m.

As the banks sector demonstrated, it is not only the profit & loss account which can suffer with changes in taxation. Table 17.3 shows the effect on gearing for those companies which would have experienced at least a 10% fall in EPS in 1993 and at least a 10% reduction in shareholders' funds as a result of a move to full provisioning for deferred tax.

Table 17.3   Companies with expected EPS fall of over 10% and more than 10% of shareholders' funds in unprovided deferred tax

| | Estimates impact on historic gearing | |
| | From | To |
Company	%	%
Arjo Wiggins	26	29
BAA	29	36
British Airways	148	214
British Gas	56	68
BP	67	78
Cable & Wireless	23	40
GKN	2	n/a
NFC	Net cash	n/a
Northern Electric	Net cash	n/a
Scottish Hydro	13	17
Severn Trent	30	36
Southern Electric	Net cash	n/a
Thames Water	32	38

Finally, if it is true that you can judge people by the company they keep, perhaps the same is true of accounting treatments. Only five companies in the FT-SE 100 Index made no use of the partial provision method of accounting for deferred tax in 1993:

Table 17.4   Companies without any deferred tax exposure and normal tax charge

| | | Unprovided deferred tax |
| | Tax Rate | /shareholder funds |
Company	%	%
General Electric	32	0
Marks & Spencer	32	0
Reuters	32	0
GUS	33	0
Wolseley	33	0

Isn't it interesting that amongst these five are some of the UK's most successful and conservatively financed large companies?

Part IV

Survival Techniques: some new hints and some old rules

18

WHAT A DIFFERENCE A WORD MAKES!

Clever people rarely do anything by accident
Anon

This chapter is not about a specific technique of accounting *per se*. It is simply about the need to read wording in accounts carefully, and in particular the need to compare accounts with previous years and query the meaning of any changes in wording or treatment. It is one of my assumptions in reading accounts that the finance directors of PLCs are rarely stupid, so that any change in accounting treatment or wording, or simply any specific form of words used is likely to have a purpose and it is as well that we know what it is.

GRAND MET AND INNTREPRENEUR

Grand Metropolitan's involvement in Inntrepreneur has presented it with many problems. Inntrepreneur was a joint venture into which Grand Met and Courage injected their pub interests, partly because of a desire to exit this sector and partly because of the 'Beer Orders' which limited the number of tied pubs which a brewer could own.

They attempted to run Inntrepreneur in a particular way. Previously pubs had either been managed or tenanted, and if they were tenanted the tenant paid a rent which was lower than the normal commercial rent on the pub. The balance of the return to the owner came from the 'tie' in which the tenant bought beer exclusively from the brewery which typically was the pub owner. The Beer Orders had broken down this system. Moreover, pub owners like Grand Met realised that it left their income from the pubs subject to the vagaries of the economic cycle as consumption of drinks went up and down.

Inntrepreneur's solution to this was to get the tenants to sign longer-term leases at higher rents so that Inntrepreneur received a rental income whatever volume of drinks was sold. This proved mightily unpopular with Inntrepreneur franchisees who claimed that Inntrepreneur had over-stated the barrelage on which the rents were based, with accompanying legal actions and disruption of the Grand Met AGM. Even apart from this, Inntrepreneur had run into problems almost immediately after its foundation as a result of the combined effect of the recession, changes in drinking habits away from beer, a surplus of brewing capacity, falling pub values in line with falling property values and the surfeit of pubs which resulted from brewers having to cut the size of their tied estate to suit the Beer Orders.

Exhibit 18.1 **Grand Metropolitan Annual Report 1992**

Inntrepreneur Estates
The group has a 50% shareholding in Inntrepreneur Estate Ltd (IEL), a joint venture company in which the group and Courage merged their former tenanted pub estate. Summarised accounts based on the audited management accounts of IEL and its subsidiaries are as follows:

Profit and loss account	Year ended 30th September 1992 £m	Year ended 30 September 1991 £m
Rental and other operating profit	209	104
Costs and sundry income	(47)	(20)
Trading profit	162	84
Profit on sale of property	13	3
Interest	(203)	(109)
Loss before taxation and property revaluation (see note I)	(22)	(25)
Attributable to group	(14)	(11)
Taxation attributable to the group	(1)	-

Balance sheet	30th September 1992 £m	30th September 1991 £m
Investment properties	1,937	2,227
Other properties	28	108
Net current (liabilities)/assets	(21)	14
	1,944	2,349
Loans from the Grand Metropolitan Group	(334)	(311)
Bank loans – three to four years	(1,275)	(1,325)
– one to two years	-	(113)
Net assets	335	600
Group share of net assets	168	300

As a result the note shows that Inntrepreneur made losses of £28m in 1992 compared with £22m in 1991. Some other features are worth noting about the information concerning Inntrepreneur in the Grand Met accounts. It had a very unusual balance sheet structure. The net assets, or shareholders' funds were only £335m in 1993 compared with property assets (the pub leases) of £1,965m. The balance of the funding for this came from a loan from Grand Met of £334m and bank loans of £1,275m. In other words, Inntrepreneur was abnormally highly geared. The reasons why the banks were willing to permit a loss-making company to carry this gearing was evident from notes (ii)-(iv) in Note 17 of the Grand Met accounts: Grand Met and Fosters (which owned Courage) had basically guaranteed Inntrepreneur's debts. However, these debts did not appear in the Grand Met group balance sheet. As a 50/50 owned joint venture, Inntrepreneur was treated as an associate and so the only figure in the Grand Met balance sheet was Grand Met's share of Inntrepreneur's net assets: £168m in 1992.

Another feature of the Note on Inntrepreneur is the valuation note in 17(i). The pubs were valued 'on the assumption that Inntrepreneur leases had been granted on all public houses.' Unfortunately they hadn't:

Exhibit 18.2 **Inntrepreneur Estates Limited Annual Report 1992**

REPORT OF THE DIRECTORS

The directors present their report together with the audited financial statements for the nine month period from 1 January 1992 to 30 September 1992. Comparatives are for the nine months from 29 March to 31 December 1991.

STRUCTURE OF THE GROUP

Inntrepreneur Estates (CPC) Limited and Inntrepreneur Estate (GL) Limited are property investment companies which own the group's core estate comprising over 6,800 investment properties principally public houses. Inntrepreneur Estates (CH) PLC own those properties which are not part of the group's core estate. Inntrepreneur Estates Limited is a joint venture between Foster's Brewing Group Limited and Grand Metropolitan PLC and both parties are 50% shareholders in the company. Grand Metropolitan Estates Limited, a subsidiary of Grand Metropolitan PLC is the managing agent for Inntrepreneur Estates Limited and is responsible for the provision of all management services to the group.

The Inntrepreneur accounts show that out of over 6,000 Inntrepreneur pubs, only 4,440 were actually on the new style leases. This might strike you as odd. It is a bit like valuing a company which owns my house on the assumption that the house has been leased to the government on a rental of £50 per square foot. Fine, except that it hasn't! It is instructive to realise that a company can include a value for its properties which is based upon an assumption which simply isn't correct. The effect when this assumption was removed is seen in the following year's accounts for Grand Met:

Exhibit 18.3   Grand Met Annual Report 1993

Note 16 Inntrepreneur Estates

The group has a 50% shareholding in Inntrepreneur Estates Ltd (IEL), a joint venture company in which the group and Courage merged their former tenanted pub estates. Summarised accounts for the year ended 30th September 1993 based on the audited management accounts of IEL and its subsidiaries are as follows:

Profit and loss account	1993 £m	1992 £m
Rental and other operating income	216	209
Costs and sundry income	(65)	(47)
Operating profit	151	162
Profit on sale of property	4	13
Interest	(173)	(203)
Loss before taxation and property revaluation (see note I)	(18)	(28)
Attributable to the group	(9)	(14)
Taxation attributable to the group	-	(1)
Balance Sheet	**1993 £m**	**1992 £m**
Investment properties	1,769	1,937
Other properties	15	28
Net current liabilities	(24)	(21)
	1,760	1,944
Loans from the Grand Metropolitan group	(360)	?(334)
Bank loans – two to three year	(1,175)	(1,275)
Net assets	225	335
Group share of net assets	113	168

Note (I) indicates that the basis of valuation no longer includes the assumption that all the pubs are on long term Inntrepreneur leases, and that there has coincidentally been a fall of £160m in the valuation. It so happens that the problems at Inntrepreneur were not critical for Grand Met and have now substantially passed. But they could have been and investors had to play detective in order to find some estimate of Grand Met's true exposure.

Another aspect of the Inntrepreneur saga also warrants attention.

Exhibit 18.4 **Grand Met Annual Report 1993**

Note 7- Interest

	1993 £m	1992 £m
On bank loans, overdrafts and other loans repayable wholly repayable within five years	184	192
On finance leases	6	7
On all other loans	72	41
	262	240
Less: Interest receivable from associates	(34)	(45)
Income from currency swaps	(36)	(62)
Other interest receivable	(49)	(39)
Interest before exceptional items	143	94
Exceptional interest charge (note 6)	22	-
	165	94

Grand Met's 1993 Annual Report shows interest receiv*able* of £119m (£34m+£36m+£49m) including £34m from associates. Contrast this with the cash flow statement which shows interest receiv*ed* of £88m: a difference of £31m. Of course, both statements are using the terminology correctly: the profit & loss account can show interest which has accrued but not been received (providing there is a reasonable expectation that it will be received) whereas the cash flow statement should only include it if and when it is received.

The difference of £31m is close to the £34m due from associates, and what was Grand Met's largest associate? None other than Inntrepreneur, to which Note 17 above shows that Grand Met had a loan of £360m outstanding in 1993. Coincidence? This interest was accrued and included in Grand Met's profit & loss account at a time when Inntrepreneur was making losses and was not paying interest to Grand Met, as shown by the increase in Grand Met's loan from £334m in 1992 to £360m in 1993 (Note 16 above). Did the Grand Met Interest Note in the accounts therefore provide an accurate picture of the interest cover? Yes, but only if you also referred to the cash flow statement: there is a world of difference between the words receivable and received.

BRITISH AEROSPACE: EXPECTED VS RECEIVABLE

British Aerospace (BAe) had a problem with two of the aircraft it manufactured: the Jetstream turboprop and the BAe 146, or the Regional Jet as it has been rechristened. They weren't selling well. So BAe decided to 'sell' the surplus aircraft to lessors such as banks and in return BAe signed a finance lease over the planes. A finance lease is one in which the lessee (BAe in this case) agrees to pay out the full capital cost of the asset plus interest over the life of the lease. In other words, the risks and rewards of ownership remained with BAe, who literally owned the aircraft at the end of the leases, including any fall in the aircrafts' value.

BAe then used these aircraft which it could not sell but on which it had completed a sale and leaseback transaction, to lease on short leases to airlines. Airlines sometimes lease aircraft on short so-called operating leases because they are starting a new route and are not sure how well it will go in terms of passenger demand, so they do not want to move straight into purchasing a new aircraft outright until the route is established. Load factors and demand also change from time to time on existing routes, and airlines are often inclined to cover these possibly temporary fluctuations by leasing aircraft on short-term operating leases. The airline industry has also been deregulated, firstly in the United States, and then in other areas such as Europe. Deregulation has broken up an oligopolistic system and opened the door to new small airlines to fly routes. Most of these airlines are not financially strong enough to own their own planes, and so turn to leases. Indeed, the whole airline industry has long struggled to produce enough cash to replace its fleets without resort to financing techniques such as leasing.

So BAe and other manufacturers have had to resort to granting operating leases on the planes they are unable to sell outright. It is BAe's accounting treatment of these transactions which is of interest:

Exhibit 18.5 **BAe's Net Lease Exposure in 1992 Accounts**

	£m
Head lease commitments	2195
less: Operating lease income receivable	704
	1491
less: estimated residual values and provisions	1311
Net estimated exposure	180

The example shows the treatment of these leases in the notes in BAe's balance sheet. The head lease commitments of £2,195m are the total amount which BAe has agreed to pay the banks on the leases it signed on the sale and leaseback of the aircraft. This liability is reduced by three items: 1) the estimated residual value of the aircraft at the end of the leases, since BAe still has the risks and rewards of ownership; 2) income *receivable* under the operating leases signed with operators of the aircraft; and 3) provisions for any residual shortfall once items 1 & 2 are deducted from BAe's total liability on the head leases. There is likely to be a shortfall because the operating leases are mostly shorter in term than the head leases: the head leases cover the period required for BAe to pay the full capital cost of the aircraft, whereas airline operators want shorter leases in order to retain the flexibility to relinquish the plane if their circumstances change. Moreover, the operating lease rates may be lower than the payments on the head leases. This shortfall was estimated in 1992 at just £180m.

Exhibit 18.6 **BAe's Net Lease Exposure in Rover Document**

	£m
Head lease commitments	1778
Third party leases	1074
	2852
less: expected sub-lease income	(1756)
expected residual values	(230)
	866
Adjustment to net present value	(213)
Net exposure provided for	653

Less than a year after the publication of the 1992 accounts, BAe had to publish a circular to shareholders on the sale of the Rover Group to BMW. The position it revealed about the aircraft leases was markedly different to the 1992 accounts. It shows that the original head lease commitments had shrunk to £1,778m, no doubt from repayments and some disposals. But a new item 'Third party leases' had appeared with a total liability of an additional £1,074m. What this represented was aircraft which BAe had 'sold' to airlines who could not afford to pay for them outright. The airlines got banks or other lessors to buy the aircraft instead and lease them to the airline, but since some of these airlines were not creditworthy enough to purchase the planes they were equally unlikely to be able to obtain lease finance. BAe therefore guaranteed the leases. In these circumstances, most people would surely not have agreed that BAe had sold the planes in any normally accepted sense.

The remainder of the note which was repeated in the 1993 accounts, showed the same deductions as before to reduce this liability: 1) estimated residual values – these were now shown separately from; 2) provisions for BAe's net exposure after these deductions which had risen to £653m; and 3) *expected* sub lease income of £1,756m. This last item had risen significantly from £704m in the 1992 accounts. Just as well, since BAe's head lease liabilities had soared with the disclosure of the third party leases guaranteed, and it was needed to offset this. Indeed, the rise may be directly connected since it may relate to operating sub lease income of the planes for which BAe had guaranteed the head leases. But what is curious is the change in wording: the sub lease income was no longer 'receivable' but just 'expected'.

What are we meant to read into this change in wording? Frankly I do not know. But 'receivable' has a firmer feel to it than 'expected'. 'Receivable' suggests that it at least relates to a sub lease which has been signed. Even then the lease income is not certain to be received – the lessee may go bust for example. But 'expected' sounds like something much less definite. Does it indicate that the BAe management had guesstimated the operating lease income from renewals after the existing operating leases, which are generally shorter than the head leases, expire? Once again, I don't know, but I feel that we need to know in order to reach an informed judgement on BAe's financial condition. After all this was not a trivial liability. The head lease liabilities were much larger than BAe's shareholders' funds.

And we must always be wary of such changes in the wording of accounts, because smart people rarely make such changes by accident.

19

SURVIVAL TECHNIQUES IN THE
ACCOUNTING JUNGLE

What a tangled web we weave
when first we practise to deceive
Sir Walter Scott

We have looked in some detail at various techniques of so-called creative accounting. Before proffering some advice on what to look for when reading a set of accounts and attempting to analyse a company's performance, perhaps we should dwell for a moment upon a common-sense definition of what it is we are looking for. As the development of this book since 1992 illustrates, this is a subject which does not stand still. There is an industry devoted to enhancing companies' reported performance and circumventing the accounting regulations, so that learning a few specific techniques to avoid will not serve you well for all time.

Instead when reading company accounts you should bear in mind that all forms of creative accounting fall into one or more of the following categories:

1. To inflate reported profits, and in particular earnings per share (by far the most obvious);

2. To report profits at the expense of the balance sheet: for example if there is a loss it is taken to reserves, or if there is a loss on an asset such as a property it is transferred to fixed assets and the write down is taken to reserves, whereas profits (even capital profits) are routed through the profit & loss account in the hope that the market will attach a PE to them;

3. Reporting profits without generating an equivalent amount of cash: even if this does not indicate that the profits are being 'created', which it often does, companies which have to use increasing quantities of fixed assets or working capital to generate their profits are unlikely to be a good investment;

4. Reporting lower borrowings: beyond a certain point debt gearing is dangerous to equity holders since it places their returns at risk, highly geared companies will often try to find a way to disguise this problem.

Try to analyse any unfamiliar accounting techniques you come across to see whether they have any of these effects.

Imagine you are faced with *your* first set of Annual Report and Accounts. How in practice should you go about avoiding the pitfalls of creative accounting?

1. Read the Accounts Backwards

Most public company Annual Report and Accounts are prepared by experts: finance directors, accountants and public relations consultants and the order in which the information appears within them is no accident. True, some of the statutory information required by the Companies Acts and the Stock Exchange listing requirements appears in a particular order, but aside from this the Annual Report and Accounts is set out so as to impress you – the potential or actual investor.

If you start at the front you will encounter the often glossy cover, the Chairman's Statement, the Review of Operations and the Director's Report not to mention the series of glossy photographs before you get to the all important Accounts, the Notes on which are often last of all. Avoid all this 'gloss'. When did you last see a Chairman's Statement that described the performance of the business in less than glowing terms?

Starting from the back of the Annual Report and Accounts and reading forwards is often more instructive. There is a lot of useful information at the back of an Annual Report. Often it contains the resolutions for the Annual General Meeting, which can provide some interesting insights into the powers the Directors want in order to allot shares etc. The last Note to the Accounts is often the Contingent Liabilities Note – a potential killer, as we have seen. Are there any guarantees to businesses sold etc?

Work towards the front through items such as the Notes, if any, on Pension Funding, noting whether the surplus has given rise to any credits in the profit and loss account or prepayment assets in the balance sheet.

Perform calculations as you go: if there is a pension fund prepayment asset, what proportion of Net Asset Value does it represent, what proportion of profits results from amortising a pension fund surplus? If pension fund credits are credited to interest and investment income what would interest cover be if they were excluded?

The Note on Interest payable or received should also be carefully scrutinised. Has interest been capitalised? If so, what would interest cover (operating profit divided by net interest paid) be if interest capitalised is included in interest payable? And so on, searching for each of the creative accounting techniques which we have described.

By the time you reach the Profit and Loss Account and Consolidated Balance Sheet, you should already have cross-referenced to them several times to make calculations which will give you a clearer picture of the company's financial health than the Chairman's Statement will.

When you reach the Profit & Loss account and the balance sheet there are further calculations to perform. For example, what are the operating profit margins (operating profit divided by sales turnover)? What is the trend in these margins: are they going up or down over time? How do they compare with the margins reported by competitors? If they are lower it may represent an opportunity *if* the management is doing something about it. But if they are higher why are they? Is it because the company has some natural competitive advantage such as lower costs, patents to protect its prices or a natural monopoly in a region? If you cannot detect the competitive advantage which has delivered the superior margins then you are more likely to be dealing with a case of creative accountancy.

The profit & loss account and the balance sheet need to be combined. What is the return on shareholders' equity and the return on capital including debt capital? Is this return adequate, or can you better it at the building society or in a risk free investment such as gilts? If so, why take the risk of buying shares? And of course remember to add back goodwill in performing this calculation.

The cash flow statement needs to be scrutinised as well. What cash flow is the company generating? Look at it at various levels in the cash flow: at the operating profit level, before and after capital expenditure, at the 'bottom line'. Compare this with the equivalent line in the profit & loss account to determine whether the company is generating the same amount of cash as it is reporting in profits. For example, is the operating profit equivalent to the operating cash flow? If not, why not? If the company is generating less cash than profit it may just be experiencing some working capital strain, but it may also be cooking the books because profits are easier to inflate artificially than cash flows.

You can see that there are a large number of calculations that you may need to perform to get a good picture of the company's financial health. Most investors and analysts who do this regularly develop a drill with a set of calculations and ratios which they routinely perform, and some additional ones which they move on to if they find something interesting.

2. Read the Accounting Policies – and compare

The Accounting Policies Note which is usually placed just before or after the Profit and Loss Account and Balance Sheet is vital and must be read carefully. If there are any changes in accounting policy it is not sufficient in assessing the company as a potential investment just to ensure that the new policies fall within Generally Accepted Accounting Practice (GAAP). This is assured if the Auditor's Report is 'clean' i.e. does not contain any qualifications, but simply states that the accounts present a 'true and fair view'. All of the techniques described in Parts II and III on Accounting Techniques fall within UK GAAP and would not have led to a qualified Auditors Report. In any case, you cannot rely upon the Auditors – you are on your own. In a 'true and fair' statement the key word is 'view' – it is just someone's opinion.

Any change in Accounting Policy must be considered in the light of the effect which it will have on profits. If it increases the profits by, for example, cutting the depreciation charge, is this reflected in the market rating of the shares compared with similar companies? What is the practice of competitors?

Nor is it sufficient just to read the current year's Accounting Policies Note – read the previous year's since some changes, such as depreciation lives, do not count as a change in Accounting Policy and do not need to be disclosed. But they can be detected by comparing policies in one year with another.

3. 'Screen' the Accounts using various 'filters'

Accounts provide many figures which can be used to screen a company's performance so as to raise questions which can be directed to the company's management, or a stockbroking research analyst, or simply to avoid investment in the company if you don't like the answer. Probably the best example of a screen from Part II on Accounting Techniques is comparing net interest income/expense with the average net cash/debt derived by averaging the figures in the company's opening and closing balance sheets. This test has many pitfalls – seasonal cash flows can make a nonsense of the calculation. *But it is only intended to pose questions, not to provide answers.* And it is worth questioning how a company such as Hanson derived net income of £178m on average net cash in 1990-91 Accounts of £454.5m. The answer may lie in seasonal cash flows, or the impact of acquisitions or disposals, or it may not, and the question is a valid one.

Another simple screen which is provided for us by an outside agency is the tax charge. The Inland Revenue has a great deal more information about a business than an investor can obtain from the Annual Report and Accounts. Taxable profits are different from accounting profits so that the tax computation is aiming for a different sort of answer, but where the tax rate varies significantly from the statutory rate, the Inland Revenue is in effect stating that it has a different view of the taxable profit of that business to the profit shown in the Accounts. For this reason a low tax charge is another good 'screen' to use for provoking the question: why does the Revenue view the company's profits as lower than the figure in the accounts?

Table 19.1   Low Tax Charge Companies*

	%
Stakis	(6.5)
Costain	(3.6)
Storehouse	10.0
Queens Moat Houses	16.9
CRH	18.7
Cable & Wireless	19.7
Rolls-Royce	20.5
Courtaulds	21.5
Hillsdown	21.8
Booker	22.1
Whitbread	24.4
Hanson	24.4
NFC	24.7
Polly Peck	14.0

* last available accounts

25 per cent is taken as a cut-off for a 'low' tax charge given a current UK Corporation Tax rate of 33 per cent. As ever, there are plenty of innocent explanations for a low tax charge: timing differences from capital allowances on capital expenditure exceeding the depreciation charge may reduce taxable profits below the reported pre-tax profits. A company may have substantial overseas operations in areas where the tax rate is below that in the UK, such as Cable & Wireless's Hong Kong Telecom subsidiary. But there are some interesting casualties of the recession in the above list, which is reproduced from the 1992 edition of this book, such as Polly Peck, which could have been avoided on this simple basis alone.

Another useful 'screen' for changes in depreciation lives and policies is to check the percentage of assets which are depreciated each year over a series of years to see if there is any change in the proportion of assets being depreciated. MTM provides a good example:

Table 19.2   MTM – Years to 31 December

	1986 £m	1987 £m	1988 £m	1989 £m	1990 £m
Tangible gross assets	17130	13653	23168	51407	131259
(of which freehold property)	(2592)	(4438)	(3496)	(6764)	(27573)
Depreciation charge for tangible assets	1057	1617	1145	1943	3377
(of which freehold property)	(51)	(55)	(36)	(52)	(162)
Depreciation/Gross Assets %	6.2	11.8	4.9	3.8	2.6
(excluding property)	(6.9)	(17.0)	(5.6)	(4.2)	(3.1)

Apart from 1987, when the figures were distorted by an acquisition, MTM's depreciation as a proportion of gross assets shows a continuous downhill trend to the point where in 1990, depreciation charged was 2½ per cent of gross assets i.e. depreciating the assets at this rate would take an average of 40 years to write down to their residual value on a straight line basis.

Depreciation of tangible assets was not the direct cause of MTM's problems, which were actually in the area of capitalising development costs to create intangible assets, but a review of the company's depreciation policies such as the calculation above would certainly have revealed an interesting trend in the accounting treatment of fixed assets and the capitalisation of costs should also have been picked up as another creative technique.

Figure 19.1   MTM Share price chart 1991–92

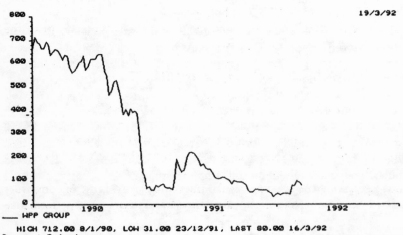

HIGH 712.00 8/1/90, LOW 31.00 23/12/91, LAST 80.00 16/3/92
Source : Datastream

The result for MTM shareholders of the auditors' final disagreement over accounting for development costs has been a catastrophic fall in the share price (see Figure 19.1).

4. Cash is king!

In the first edition of this book a section of this Survival Techniques chapter was devoted to the concept of cash flow, and in particular the new Financial Reporting Standard 1 which had just been introduced. This subject now warrants a chapter of its own, and Chapter 8 covers Cash Flow Accounting and outlines the way in which even cash flow statements produced under the auspices of FRS 1 can still be misleading.

However, for the reader attempting to survive and preserve his or her money the advice remains the same. Profits can be manufactured by creative accounting but creating cash flow is at least more difficult, and in anything other than the short term it is impossible. Profits are after all the result of the accountants' 'true and fair *view*'. In other words an opinion. Whereas cash is a fact. And cash is ultimately more important than profits. It pays the dividends and lack of cash is the reason businesses fail.

But as Chapter 8 above emphasises, it is not enough simply to look at the cash flow statement. It too needs to be analysed. When I was touring institutional investors to talk about BTR (see page 32) one of the retorts I frequently received was "Ah, but BTR generates cash". This statement in itself is almost meaningless. How much cash was BTR producing? The same as its profits (taken at an equivalent point in the cash flow statement and profit & loss account: it is no use comparing operating cash flow with retained profits), or more or less? What return on capital did the cash flow represent? Were the cash flows generated by repeatable items such as operating profits, or was the company squeezing working capital, or making disposals for cash which could not be repeated?

Cash flow needs as much thought and analysis as any other part of the accounts before it will yield its answers.

5. Who says you can't predict corporate failure?

Faced with the rash of corporate failures amongst quoted companies in recent years, many investors just shrug their shoulders and seem to accept that 'some you win some you lose'. Nonsense. I hope the ability to spot corporate failures in the widest sense has been demonstrated by the history of this book and the aftermath of its publication in 1992 (see pages 6–8). I am not just talking about corporate failure in the narrow sense of companies which go into administration, but also those whose share price performance is catastrophic once their true results become apparent, such as the Queens Moats and Tiphooks of this world. Even the Grand Met and BTR share price performances since 1992 could have had a serious effect on your wealth.

But the ironic point is that investors can avoid them. Apart from the sort of fundamental financial analysis which I advocate, there are proprietary systems which successfully assess corporate financial strength and weakness.

One such is Syspas, a system which looks at companies' financial ratios and scores them on a weighted combination of those ratios. This system was devised by Professor Richard Taffler from City University and it has an extraordinary track record at predicting corporate failure. At its foundation is a principle of so-called multivariate analysis: that a company's performance needs to be assessed by a combination of ratios. When companies realise that their performance is being assessed by a single figure, such as the ubiquitous earnings per share, or that their financial safety is being assessed simply by balance sheet gearing, for example, then they have the capacity to change that ratio by the use of creative accounting. But it is possible to devise a combination of ratios such that 'fixing' one will cause another to deteriorate. Hence the need for multivariate analysis, and hence the quote from Sir Walter Scott at the beginning of this chapter. Liars are often caught out because elements of their story do not tally. Companies are no different.

An example of the Syspas analysis is shown in the Queens Moat chart:

Figure 19.2 The Risk Profile of Queens Moat Houses

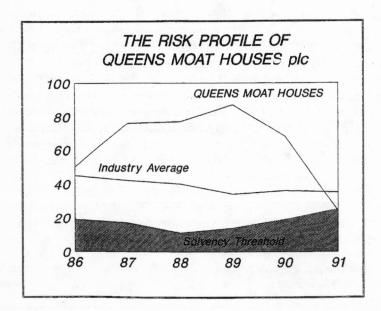

It shows the score for Queens Moat based upon the weighted combination of Syspas ratios compared with other quoted companies to produce a percentile score over time. At the beginning of the chart in 1986, Queens Moat's score was close to 50, i.e. it was an average quoted company in terms of financial strength and weakness. The chart has two other lines: The Industry Average showing the average Syspas score for the industry in which Queens Moat operates – in this case hotels; and the Solvency Threshold – once a company's score drops below this line, the experience of the Syspas multivariate analysis shows that it is at risk of financial failure.

Queens Moat's Syspas score started to drop in 1989, and by the time the 1991 results were announced in April 1992 it was descending below the Solvency Threshold and was clearly at risk. This risk subsequently became a reality when Queens Moat collapsed requiring a financial reconstruction which all but wiped out the ordinary shareholders' equity.

It was possible to predict that Queens Moat was likely to get into difficulty from the numerous examples of creative accounting shown in the previous chapters which are taken from its accounts. It was also possible to predict it from an objective numerical analysis like Syspas. Yet most financial commentators were oblivious as the commentary in the Lex column of the *Financial Times* on the 1991 results shows:

> It was a pity Queens Moat's poor presentation of two relatively minor matters distracted attention yesterday from a fine performance last year. In marking its shares down by 5 per cent, the market concentrated on a surprisingly fully priced but small UK acquisition and a confusing stance on depreciation policy. But as Forte's forthcoming results will doubtless confirm, Queens Moat managed a significantly better trading result than its peers.
>
> The reasons for the mere 4 per cent fall in annual pre-tax profits were evident at the interim stage last August. The continental European hotels, particularly in Germany, grew fast enough to offset most of the effects of recession in the UK. Granted, the UK business was hard enough hit for the group's self-employed managers to negotiate a 6 per cent fall in their annual contributions. But on the other hand, that should allow UK profits to recover more strongly when the market eventually improves, although more than half of future revenues will be generated in Europe. On a forward multiple of just 10, the shares look better value than Forte. But given the sector's abiding lack of fashion among investors, that scarcely amounts to a ringing endorsement.
>
> *Lex Column, Financial Times*
> *April 1992*

Lex is arguably the elite of financial journalism in the UK, yet it had the blind spot for Queens Moat's failure in common with most analysts following the company. There were plenty of analysts' Buy circulars which accompanied the 1991 results. Looking back at what was wrong with the accounts we can now see how shoddy this 'analysis' was.

Nor is Queens Moat an isolated example of the ability of objective analysis to spot impending financial problems. Tiphook was one of the stars of the first edition of this book. The Syspas analysis at that time showed that it had hardly ever been solvent:

Figure 19.3   The Risk Profile of Tiphook plc

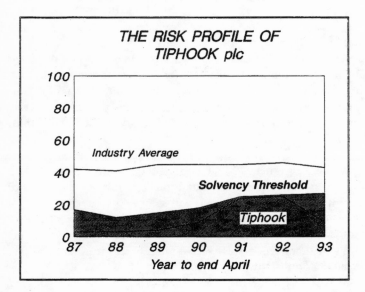

Nor are these systems only valid for companies which fail. As well as the many accounting issues which I had over BTR in 1993/4 I was not unimpressed by the effect the Hawker Siddeley acquisition had on its risk profile (see Figure 19.3).

Although it had clawed its way back, the Hawker Siddeley acquisition had clearly damaged BTR's financial strength, a theme which is common to every form of analysis I applied at that time. But it was not until 1994 that the stock market managed to discern this.

In my view the problem is not whether it is truly possible to spot creative accountancy, or whether financial weakness and failure can be detected by a systematic approach. The problem lies not in devising this analysis, but rather in the human inability to accept objectivity. Compare and contrast the accounting analysis of BTR and the Syspas assessment in 1993 with the fund managers I saw who said "But it's a good company". A bit woolly, that.

Figure 19.3   BTR PLC

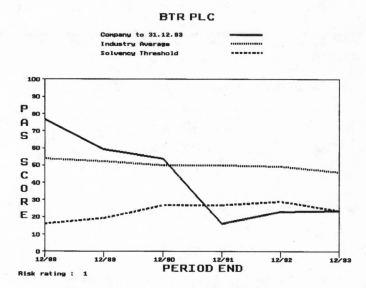

I intend to return to this subject in more detail in my next book, *Corporate Pathology*. But until then, safe investing.

6. If in doubt, don't invest

It should by now be evident that you as an investor are on your own. None of the techniques which have been described are in breach of UK GAAP so the auditors will not warn you about them. Investors who believe that the way to prevent their losses from corporate collapses and creative accountancy piling up is to tighten standards of auditing would appear to be sadly mistaken given the evidence to date!

How about help from the analytical community? Most stockbroking analysis would seem to have focused upon the 'magic' Earnings per Share figure and ignored the wider issues of creative accounting used to generate that figure. Once again, historical precedent at least would suggest that in general investors will not get much help from this quarter.

The investor must perform his own analysis. Much of the analysis I have described in this book will lead to questions rather than answers. These questions should be posed directly to the company. Institutional investors have many opportunities for this, but small investors can ask questions at the AGM, write to the Finance Director or ask their stock broker the questions. If the answer is not satisfactory in terms of allaying the investor's concern that creative accounting is in use then the best solution is not to invest. This is your only effective sanction, not writing to your M. P. about standards of auditing.

Professional punters in other areas of investment have long realised this is their only solution:

> Not to bet until the odds be considered fair, reasonably or completely in the favour of the backer is an advantage which must never be surrendered. The bookmaker has to lay odds all the time for each and every race – but the backer can choose if and when to bet. (*Braddocks Complete Guide to Horse Race Selection and Betting.*)

APPENDIX I

COLOROLL

Coloroll came to the market in mid-1985 with sales of £37m and profits of a little under £4m. Over the next four years growth was dramatic, with sales reaching £565m and profits £56m. However, in mid-1990 administrative receivers were appointed. The shares, originally issued at 135p, soared to 385p in 1987 but were suspended at under 10p just five years after flotation. At its peak the group's stock market value was £424m.

The main cause of failure was the over-rapid expansion of the group, particularly the massive acquisition programme. As the table shows, in just four years and starting with a market value of £37m, Coloroll acquired companies costing over £400m (around £270m net of disposals).

Coloroll: The main deals

Date		Deals	Value £m	Sales turnover £m
1985	April	Flotation	37	37
1986	June	Acq of Worley (wallcoverings)	2	4
	June	Acq of Biltons (ceramics)	5	9
	July	Acq of Alexander Drew (fabric printing)	3	4
	July	Rights Issue	13	–
	August	Acq of Staffordshire Potteries	14	25
1987	Feb	Acq of Fogarty (home furnishings)	31	40
	March	Acq of Cartwright & Edwards (ceramics)	3	6
	March	Acq of Wallpapers Inc	10	23
	March	Acq of Wallbridge Carpets	9	18
	March	Acq of Crown House (glass & tableware)	87	207
	June	Sale of Packaging Div	6	n/a
	Sept	Sale of Crown House Engineering	36	150
1988	June	Acq of John Crowther Group	215	358
	Aug	Sale Crowther Cloth & clothing	93	159
	Sept	Acq of William Barrett (furniture)	15	24
	Sept	Acq of Texture Tex (carpet yarns)	4	13
1989	Jan	Acq of Burlington (wall coverings)	7	11

It is likely that the main problems came with the £215m purchase of Crowther in June 1988. However, even before this there were signs that acquisition and merger accounting techniques were being exploited by Coloroll to enhance profits to the detriment of its balance sheet.

Goodwill and acquisition provisions

Coloroll wasted no time in issuing its newly quoted shares. In the year to March 1987 the accounts show that £78m (largely in shares) was spent on acquisitions and £57m was written off as goodwill. The largest of these deals was Fogarty which cost £31m. Fogarty's published accounts showed net assets in excess of £12m, suggesting goodwill of £19m. However, Coloroll's accounts show goodwill relating to this purchase of £26m. For Staffordshire Potteries, which cost £14m with published net assets of £7m, Coloroll wrote-off £11m as goodwill.

These differences are likely to be explained by heavy provisioning on acquisition. Indeed the 1987 Coloroll accounts show for the first time £11m 'other provisions' arising on acquisitions, none of which was charged to the P&L. £2m of these were utilised during the year. By comparison, Coloroll's reported profits were £10m. These 'other provisions' were subsequently (in 1988 accounts) identified as 'costs of reorganisation of subsidiaries acquired and business segments closures'.

In 1988 goodwill write-offs and acquisitions provisions were again a prominent and worrying feature of the accounts. £77m goodwill was written off reserves of which £69m related to the purchase of Crown House. This was a surprisingly large sum given that the original cost of Crown House of some £84-90m was reduced by around to £35m by disposals of some of Crown's businesses during the year (i.e. the cost net of disposals was only some £50m). Coloroll made £22m 'other provisions' on acquisition: only £1m was charged to the P&L and £22m was utilised during 1987/88. By comparison declared profits were £26m. The following table shows these provisions' movements over the two years. While the exact nature of these is unknown, it is likely that at least some of the costs and writedowns would have been charged to the P&L under a more conservative accounting régime.

Coloroll: Provisions & Profits

£m	Other provisions+	Declared pre-tax profit
Opening March 1986	Nil	
Arising on acquisition	11	
Charged to P&L	–	
Utilised in year	-2	10
Opening March 1987	9	
Arising on acquisition	22	
Charged to P&L	1	
Utilised in year	-22	26
Opening March 1988	10	

+ Provisions 'comprise costs of reorganisation of subsidiaries acquired & business segments closures'.

The John Crowther acquisition

Although there were doubts over the quality of profits in 1986/87 and 1987/88, the balance sheet at March 1988 was still relatively healthy with debt/equity of some 20 per cent (34 per cent if finance leases were included). Trading conditions were in general buoyant, acquisitions had been made largely with shares (the price of which soared in 1986 and early 1987) and substantial disposals had been made for cash. However, the Crowther deal, partly because of its sheer size, had a market impact on the balance sheet. The main problems arose from the following:

• The history of Crowther

• Continued exploitation of acquisition accounting

• Consolidation of acquired debt

• Off balance sheet debt and guarantees

An unstable acquisition?

Crowther was itself the product of mass acquisition with some 25 deals taking sales from £7m to £350m over the four years to 1987. It is likely that neither management structures nor reporting controls had been fully established in all the subsidiaries – or at least tested in a recession. The size in turnover terms and the cost (£215m) were large in relation to Coloroll and posed significant risks in the event of a downturn in trading.

Further use of acquisition accounting

The accounting treatment of the acquisition of Crowther was remarkable. Crowther was acquired for £215m in cash and shares but by the time the assets appeared to Coloroll's accounts a total of £224m – more than the original cost – had been written off as goodwill.

The documents issued in April 1988 indicate that immediately before acquisition, Crowther had net assets of around £70m, suggesting in normal circumstances goodwill of £215m minus £70m = £145m. However, by the time Coloroll's next set of accounts was published (for the year to March 1989) the total cost of the deal had effectively been raised by £75m to £290m through 'incidental' costs, stock and debtor write offs, redundancy and reorganisation costs and other items. These costs and adjustments are shown in the table:

Coloroll: Crowther acquisition cost adjustments

	£m
Original cost	215
'Incidental' costs	11
Stock & debtor write downs	10
Redundancy & relocation costs	20
Loss on disposals	10
Other write downs & payments	24
	290
Net assets of Crowther	66
Goodwill written off	224

Write downs of stock and debtors in this way easily enhance reported profits. Redundancy and relocation costs should normally be charged to pre-tax profits as exceptional items, rather than extraordinary items, where they relate to businesses which are ongoing.

In 1989 Coloroll established provisions of £56m relating to acquisitions, most of which were part of the £75m 'extra' goodwill noted above. Of these £52m were utilised during 1988/89 thereby effectively reducing costs which would otherwise be seen in the P&L account (probably as exceptional or extraordinary items). This compares with the total group's pre-tax profits of just £56m that Coloroll declared for the year.

Assumed debt

As a result of its acquisitions over 1988/89, of which Crowther was the largest, not only did Coloroll pay out cash of £39m but it also had to assume debt of some £96m. The need to assume this level of debt was far from obvious for Coloroll – or Crowther – shareholders at the time of the proposed deal in the first half of 1988.

£96m was considerably larger than the £26m debt shown for Crowther alone in the statement of proforma combined net assets in Coloroll's listing particulars dated April 1988. This used Crowther's December 1987 balance sheet. By March 1988 notes in the same document suggested that Crowther's debt had risen to £67m and seasonal influences would have played a significant part in this increase. However, it is likely that the 1987 Crowther accounts included two recent acquisitions, McCalls (US) and Homfray Carpets (Australia) as 'investments' for balance sheet purposes thereby not consolidating debt of £35m. Crowther, through an ingenious structure, held only 50 per cent of the common stock and units of these two very highly geared companies (hence qualifying for non-consolidation of balance sheets) but did have 100 per cent of the 'partially participating preferred' stock and units for P&L purposes.

All this and its implications might have been divined by the earnest reader of the listing particulars, but it would not have been easy. The 60-page complex document included not only information on Coloroll and Crowther, but was further complicated by information on Crown House, acquired by Coloroll almost a year earlier.

The status of McCalls under Coloroll was never clearly indicated – it filed for voluntary protection under Chapter 11 of the US bankruptcy code in December 1988. There was however no recourse to Coloroll in this case. Homfray Carpets (Australia) almost certainly became a true subsidiary of Coloroll but was to cause further unease later on.

The effect of the consolidation of the acquired debt, together with the goodwill write-offs and the cash element of the extra costs of the Crowther acquisition, had a marked impact on Coloroll's balance sheet. Despite disposals with a beneficial cash effect of some £90m during 1988/89, Coloroll's net debt soared to £85m and debt/equity at March 1989 rose to around 100 per cent. (This includes finance leases as debt but excludes convertible preference from equity and debt.) Trading conditions would become aggressively more difficult over the next year: Coloroll was ill equipped in balance sheet terms to cope with this.

Contingent liabilities & guarantees

In the second half of 1988, in an attempt to reduce borrowings, Coloroll agreed to dispose of the cloth and clothing divisions of Crowther. The divisions were sold to a management buy-out for a total £93m. The consideration was a complex mixture of £53m cash, £21m of debt being sold on by Coloroll, the issue to Coloroll as vendor of £8m nominal redeemable preference shares, £10m of subordinated loan notes and £1m of shares of the MBO equity called the Response Group.

The redeemable preference shares and the loan notes carried a yield of 12 per cent, although this was payable by way of a premium on redemption. Coloroll sold on these securities to realise cash of approximately £18m, but the sale was 'subject to recourse to Coloroll in certain circumstances'. This liability appeared as a note in the March 1989 Coloroll accounts as a contingent liability, totalling by then £22m.

Another disposal which did not isolate Coloroll from the underlying debt was that of Homfray Carpets (Australia). This sale, again to a management buy-out, was approved in late April 1989 but was reflected as complete in Coloroll's March 1989 balance sheet. The A$42m deal was structured in a complex but by now familiar way: AS$19m repayment of intercompany debt, the issue to the vendors of a A$7m loan note and only A$16m of direct cash. Additionally, a 26 per cent stake in the MBO was retained by Coloroll.

Moreover, Coloroll had guaranteed 'borrowings and other bank facilities' of Homfray with a note in the 1989 accounts indicating that these were equivalent to £15m at the time.

Coloroll also guaranteed borrowings of over £4m of a purchaser of land from the group during 1988/89.

Window dressing

By March 1989 the group's gearing had increased substantially, but the formal consolidated balance sheet was presented in such a way as to suggest on initial reading that debt was around £67m and capital plus reserves was around £102m. This was a high – but not excessive – ratio.

Further detailed examination of the notes to the accounts showed that this debt figure excluded short-term debentures (issued for payment of an acquisition) and finance leases, both of which unlike bank loans had not been separated out of 'other creditors'. Moreover, bills of exchange had increased from almost nil to £6m. Capital included for the first time 'guaranteed redeemable convertible cumulative preference stock' repayable in 1997 at a premium if not converted. Moreover, equity reserves had been boosted by an asset revaluation in the year – something that would have normally been carried out during 'fair value' adjustments on consolidation of acquisitions.

The balance sheet for March 1989 could be redrafted to suggest debt/equity over 100 per cent before any consideration of contingent liabilities as shown in the table.

Coloroll: Restatement of debt & equity for March 1989

	Debt £m		Capital & Reserves £m
Net bank debt as shown	67	Capital & reserves as shown	102
Add debentures	7	Less convertible pref	18
Add finance leases	11	Less revaluation surplus	9
Total debt	*85		75

* Excludes contingent liabilities, mainly debt guarantees, of £40m.

The final stage

The crystallisation of the contingent liabilities associated with some of the disposals was probably one of the key events leading to the downfall of the entire group.

Trading conditions deteriorated rapidly through 1989. The interim results showed profit halved and a trading statement in January 1990 warned of second half profits materially below the first. Debt had risen to around £150m by January 1990 with the group bearing the costs of restructuring and integration of acquisitions – and much higher working capital. The contingent liabilities – mainly associated with the guarantees of loans to the Response Group and Homfray Carpets (Australia) – were now £40m. The appointment of a receiver at the Response Group and deteriorating conditions in Australia meant that total potential debt was thus heading towards £200m, while the true equity base after further write-offs was probably lower than the £80m in March 1989 accounts. (These accounts were showing Coloroll's residual holdings in Response and Homfray at £9m.)

The preference dividend was passed in March 1990.

Refinancing proposals were discussed through May but were unsuccessful. Administrative receivers were appointed in the following month.

APPENDIX II

BRITISH & COMMONWEALTH

British & Commonwealth has yet to be finally buried, largely because the mess at Atlantic Computers, which brought the group down in May 1990, has still to be sorted out. At the time of writing a judicial decision on the OTI's request to ban certain B&C and Atlantic directors from becoming company directors again is still awaited. Although Atlantic was the final nail in the coffin, and is often referred to as a 'deal too far', B&C would have been a pretty sickly mess, even without the massive liability bequeathed by Atlantic.

At its peak in 1987 B&C was capitalised at just under £2bn and was the 46th largest FTSE-100 stock.

Personality cult

The personality of John Gunn was very much at the heart of B&C. Small in stature, but with a strong and colourful personality, he was very much a product of Thatcher's Britain and was rarely out of the business sections of the Press. Starting his business career as a foreign exchange trader at Barclays, he made his name at Exco, the moneybroking empire he built from a £5.2m management buyout in 1979 and of which he was chief executive until he resigned in September 1985. By this time Exco was worth £510m, having been floated on the Stock Exchange in 1981 for £56m. The buyout had been backed by the original British & Commonwealth Shipping Company who also backed Gunn in the build-up of Telerate in which Exco had a 52 per cent stake. From an investment at minimal cost, Exco sold its stake in Telerate for £360m and it was over the question of what to do with the proceeds of this sale that Gunn resigned from Exco.

Nevertheless, it was the success of Exco, whose pre-tax profits rose from £9m in 1981 to £21.6m in 1985, and the Telerate deal in particular, which endowed Gunn with a King Midas reputation. This is very important to the understanding of future events at B&C which Gunn joined as an executive director after he resigned from Exco in September 1985. He then became chairman at the end of 1986. The announcement of both events had the effect of boosting B&C's share price significantly in anticipation of great things ahead. In the end it took just three years to turn an asset-rich if sleepy commercial services conglomerate into a rag-bag of financial services companies supported by a balance sheet with borrowings of £1.8bn and a net tangible deficit of £300m in the last published accounts at the end of 1989. The excesses which led to this situation were clearly encouraged by the raging bull market prior to October 1987. But long afterwards, the question of the goodwill and level of debt on B&C's balance sheet were never given the attention they should have received, until it was too late.

The major deals

It was perhaps John Gunn's reputation that led the market to give B&C the benefit of the doubt whenever there was any. Because the group had a venture capital arm which took stakes in a whole range of companies from Anglia Secure Homes to Midland and Scottish Resources, B&C gave the impression of being more hyperactive than it actually was. The list of deals is nonetheless a fairly staggering one over such a short space of time in itself says much about the corporation excesses of the 1980s.

B&C major deals

Date	Deal	Company	%	Consideration £m
Nov 85	Sale	Exco	22	109
Nov 86	Bid	Exco	100	637
Dec 86	Bid	Steel Bros	55	45
Jun 87	Purchase	B&C shares	27	427
Aug 87	Sale	Country & New Town	44	45
Aug 87	Bid	Mercantile House	100	567
Jan 88	Bid	Abaco	100	188
Jun 88	Sale	Bricom	78	348
Jul 88	Bid	Atlantic Computers	100	410
Aug 89	Sale	Marshalls	100	160
Aug 89	Sale	Woodchester	31	67
Nov 89	Sale	Gartmore	100	155
Dec 89	Sale	Woodchester	29	49

Before looking at some of B&C's deals individually, it is worth quoting from B&C's strategy statement in January 1987. This said that 'Funding of subsidiaries and associates will be more centralised with greater emphasis on regular reporting of P&L, cash flow and balance sheets'. Hindsight permits a wry smile at this statement but in fact there appears to have been little central control. Instead, there appears to have been an obsession for doing the next deal and very little day-to-day control of the operating businesses from the centre. Indeed, it is worth repeating the point made in the introduction that B&C might just have survived the Atlantic debacle had all the previous deals been soundly based and if B&C had adhered to its own strategy statement. It should be remembered that B&C paid £416m for Atlantic in July 1988. The previous December B&C's accounts showed shareholders' funds of £1.34bn, so although the demise of Atlantic would have been extremely painful, it would not necessarily have been fatal had everything else been well. But it wasn't.

The Exco acquisition

John Gunn's first major deal was well received and gave little hint of the problems ahead apart from one aspect which was completely ignored at the time.

The £637m B&C paid for Exco was equivalent to 265p a share. Exco then owned London Forfaiting and had a cash pile of £322m, thanks to the sale of the Telerate stake. In 1987 moneybroking made pre-tax profits of £44.7m and London Forfaiting £16.5m. Thus, on a 35 per cent tax charge and after allowing for the £322m cash pile, B&C paid £315m for net profits of just under £30m in 1987 – a reasonable P/E of around 10. So far, so good. B&C had acquired a strong cash flow and Exco's cashpile provided the ammunition to develop the group into a financial services conglomerate.

The only aspect of the deal that might have caused concern was that when Gunn joined the B&C board in September 1985, the first move thereafter was the sale by B&C of its 21.6 per cent in Exco held as a result of backing the 1979 buyout. The stake was sold at 215p a share, 50p below the price at which B&C launched their bid for the whole of Exco only 13 months later. The inference here is a lack of long-term strategic thinking. There may also have been a hint of an addiction to deal-making as an end in itself which could have been levelled at B&C with more justification a year or two later.

The Caledonia share buy-in

In June 1987 the next deal came from an unexpected source when B&C announced that it was to buy in for cancellation 90m shares representing 26 per cent of the total for £427m, equivalent to 475p a share. The shares were part of the 32 per cent stake held by Caledonia Investments, the vehicle through which the Cayzer family had exercised effective control over the old B&C for years. B&C paid Caledonia £100m in cash and issued £327m preference shares which were to be repaid in equal instalments from 1988 to 1991 covered by a bank guarantee, but one which carried a rising coupon which would cost B&C £14m a year.

For the Cayzers, this was an excellent deal; the way it was structured enabled them to cash in the majority of their investment in B&C free of capital gains tax and their capital repayments were guaranteed by Barclays Bank. For B&C, the benefits were less clear. The commitment to pay £105m (including ACT) a year for four years in capital redemption plus £14m p.a. interest on the new preference shares helped to complete the deadly triangle when Atlantic's profits proved to be illusory and the disposal programme failed to go according to plan. At the time, no-one paid much attention to the cash-flow implications of the deal, which was viewed as welcome because it removed the influence of the Cayzers whose significant minority might have slowed down the transition of B&C into a financial services group. Also, despite paying out £100m in cash, B&C still had £350m of cash or near cash with which to develop the group.

Mercantile House

In July 1987, B&C announced an agreed £490m bid for Mercantile House, Exco's main moneybroking rival which also owned Alexanders Laing & Cruickshank (ALC) and Oppenheimer, the US fund manager which managed $10bn of funds (ten per cent in UK unit trusts). It was Oppenheimer that attracted B&C because it was complementary to Gartmore, its existing UK fund management operation. B&C had already agreed to sell ALC to Crédit Lyonnais and in due course planned to sell the operations of Marshalls (moneybrokers) and Williams Street (US government bond brokers).

A potential rival bid from Quadrex forced B&C to increase the value of its bid to £567m in August 1987 and the offer went unconditional a few weeks before the stock market crash. Consideration was via the issue of new shares and convertible preference shares. As part of the revised bid, Quadrex had apparently agreed to buy Marshalls and William Street for £280m, but after the crash it failed to complete the agreement (the resulting litigation has yet to be concluded). Marshalls was eventually sold to the management for £160m, William Street proved unsaleable, and after deducting the £36m paid for ALC, B&C ended up paying a net £371m for $10bn (£6.4bn) of funds under management or a very pricey 5.8 per cent of funds.

As well as the question of price, there was the matter of goodwill which represented most of the purchase price and still amounted to around £350m after the sale of Marshalls and nearly £600m when the Exco acquisition was taken into account. Although B&C opted to write off the goodwill in a straight line over 25 years (the 1988 amortisation charge was £41.9m) this method clearly overstated the worth of B&C's assets, particularly when the price paid reflected the inflated pre-crash market.

Abaco

The acquisition of Abaco was B&C's next move and further stoked up the goodwill carried on B&C's balance sheet. Abaco had been a 26 per cent associate of B&C since 1986 and was engaged primarily in insurance broking, loss adjusting and estate agency – all 'people businesses'. B&C's offer in December 1987 for the remainder of the share capital at 69p a share valued Abaco at £186m, yet as at 30 June 1987, Abaco had shareholders' funds of only £507,000 and EPS in the year to June 1987 were only 2.3p a share. It is not surprising that after the acquisition, B&C injected £30m of new capital into Abaco. This, plus the cash element of the bid, removed £106m from B&C's cash pile.

Abaco's pre-tax profit in 1987 was £6.5m but the offer document stated that the results did 'not reflect the earnings capacity of the business as (then) constituted because of the large number of significant acquisitions completed during the year and since the year end'. Abaco's own accounts would make an interesting case study, but suffice it to say that the subsequent collapse of the housing market meant the earnings capacity was never realised, leaving B&C with another £150m of pretty useless goodwill on its balance sheet.

The Bricom buyout

B&C's balance sheet problems were compounded by the sale of a majority stake in Bricom to the management in July 1988 for £398m. Bricom contained the commercial and service activities of the old B&C. Apart from property worth in the region of £100m, Bricom represented virtually all the tangible assets of B&C. On the surface, the P/E of 19.6 looked a good deal for B&C, but the £30.5m pre-tax profits reported in 1987 really did understate the earnings potential of the group and the conservative accounting used over the years for what had been the heart of B&C under the Cayzer family's management had also understated the asset value of the group. At Bristow Helicopters, for example, one of Bricom's subsidiaries, the fleet was depreciated over eight years against a typical life of 25 years – hardly accounting for growth!

B&C retained a 22 per cent stake in Bricom. Using its cash flow and disposal proceeds, Bricom repaid over half its acquisition loan within 18 months and the 1990 medium-term loan was repaid a year early. When, 20 months after the buyout, B&C sold most of its residual stake to Bricom's other institutional shareholders for £21.6m, B&C proudly announced the value of its investment had doubled. What a pity it only held 22 per cent of the equity! The ultimate twist came just before the final demise of B&C when Bricom, now debt free, was sold to a Swedish buyer for £338m.

Atlantic Computers

Meanwhile, B&C had made what proved to be its fifth major acquisition having also built up a 60 per cent interest in Woodchester Investments, the Irish leasing company, through market purchases and capital injections for a total cost of around £35m. The agreed £416m bid for Atlantic was announced barely a month after the Bricom deal and added another £350m of goodwill to the balance sheet, bringing the total to around £1.5bn which exceeded shareholders' funds by around £300m at the end of 1988. Thus, with a net tangible deficit of £300m and total borrowings of £1.8bn at the end of 1988, B&C never really had a chance once its operating profits began to be hit by the downturn in financial services. The accounting treatment of Atlantic's profits was found to have exaggerated them hugely, as discussed in Chapter 9 on Contingent Liabilities. The bottom line here was that B&C had to write off £550m against the £416m acquisition cost of Atlantic less than two years after it was made.

Holed below the water line

However, as referred to earlier, B&C's balance sheet was already in a sickly state before Atlantic went under. There was no question of dubious accounting here because all this was in the balance sheet as outlined below. What is not clear is that the goodwill carried from B&C's acquisitions was far too high in relation to the then current worth of the businesses. We have outlined these major acquisitions earlier and whereas the Exco deal was a good one in price terms and strategic logic, B&C paid far too much with the benefit of hindsight for Mercantile House, Abaco and Atlantic. The errors were compounded by the sale of Bricom at what turned out to be something of a bargain price for the buyers.

British & Commonwealth debt position

31 December	1988	1988	1989 est	1989 est
	£m	£m	£m	£m
Debt repayable within one year				
Bank overdrafts and loans	−472.0		−102	
Cash	272.4			
Caledonia Pref shares	−81.9		−81.9	
Debt repayable after more than one year		−281.5		−183.9
Fixed loans and overdrafts	−621.1		−621.1	
7.75% CULS	−320.5		−320.5	
10.5% unsecured loan stock 23012	−231.4		−231.4	
Other	−96.4		−96.4	
Caledonia Pref shares	−245.6		−163.7	
	−1515.0		−1413.1	
Total borrowings		**−1796.5**		**−1617.0**
Less liquid investments		265.9		160.0
Total borrowings		−1530.6		−1453.0

1989 cash in		1989 cash out	
Marshalls sale	£160m	Caledonia pref (inc ACT)	£105m
Woodchester sale	£67m	ESOP	£50m
Portfolio sales	£120m est	Dividend payments	£34m
		Advance to BCMB	£60m
	£347m		£249m

Without Atlantic, B&C could have made around £60m pre-tax in 1990, but after tax, preference dividends and minorities this would have left attributable profits of only £18m. Thus, if the group had maintained the dividend at 9.25p at a cost of £33m, the 1990 Caledonia preference share repayment of £105m would have led to a cash outflow of around £120m. On top of the existing debt mountain this means that B&C would have had no option but to start selling the family silver such as Gartmore. Once this started to occur, there really was no future for B&C.

Ignoring the warning signs

It cannot be said that the market entirely ignored B&C's problems because the shares fell from a peak of 565p in 1987 to well below 100p before the final disaster occurred. However, a number of commentators were seeking to explain away B&C's debt despite it being clearly exposed in the accounts, and few people seriously questioned the value of B&C's goodwill or considered the cash-flow implications of the Caledonia deal and the interest bill on the mounting debt.

It was cash flow as much as anything which killed B&C, but we must finish with Atlantic and the signal which proved to be the thin end of the accounting wedge. In B&C's 1989 interim statement, barely 12 months after Atlantic became a subsidiary of the group, the following paragraph appeared:

> The pattern of investment in computer technology is changing rapidly and Atlantic has responded by further improving its leasing strategy and its lease portfolio management techniques. Accordingly, Atlantic's lease portfolio is being reviewed as part of our assessment of the fair value of the businesses acquired and appropriate provisions will be made as necessary. This review is not expected to have material impact on Atlantic's continuing growth or on the group's 1989 earnings.

In retrospect, this turned out to be the most potent warning of all.

APPENDIX III

POLLY PECK

On 3 September 1990 Polly Peck announced record interim results for the six months to 30 June 1990 and made enthusiastic comments on prospects for the year and beyond. On 20 September 1990 the shares were suspended at 108p following a Serious Fraud Office raid on a private company associated with Polly Peck's Chairman, Chief Executive and 25 per cent shareholder Asil Nadir. After a further month of negotiations with its banks Polly Peck was placed in administration on 25 October 1990.

The rise

In 1980 Asil Nadir took control of a small UK textiles company, Polly Peck, which enjoyed spectacular share price performance following the injection and development of his Cyprus/Turkey assets. While the general direction was up, performance was volatile with both the existence and profitability of the assets under constant question, as was the relationship with other Nadir vehicles. In the mid 1980s the shares suffered a major setback. Profits growth slowed, City expectations were disappointed and after a period of isolation a number of key senior management appointments were made.

At the start of 1989 Polly Peck was capitalised at around £700m and comprised two main business areas, food and electronics, with two smaller operations in leisure and textiles – the former expanding, the latter contracting. Both food and electronics were based in Cyprus and Turkey although a number of acquisitions had been made in Europe, the USA and the Far East in an attempt to expand the geographical spread of the group. This strategy was only partially successful and a stagnant share price was unsettled by a number of management departures.

All this changed in September 1989 when Polly Peck bought Del Monte, the USA fresh food group, for £560m partially funded by a £280m rights issue at 245p, and in October a 51 per cent stake in Sansui, a quoted Japanese electronics company for £69m. Both Del Monte and Sansui operated in activities where Polly Peck had considerable experience and both added strong brand names and international exposure.

Amid widespread talk of synergy benefits the share price performed strongly at the end of 1989 and into 1990 and entered the FTSE 100 with a peak market capitalisation of over £1.5bn. This strength was maintained by anticipation of further corporate activity designed both to reduce debt and to ensure the share price reflected the true value of its underlying businesses, statements formally repeated in the April 1990 report and accounts.

The first restructuring took place in May 1990 when Polly Peck injected its Far Eastern electronics operations into Sansui, taking its stake from 51 per cent to 70 per cent, and floated a minority stake in its Turkish electronics operation, Vestel, on the Istanbul stock exchange. This provided a market valuation for all of the electronics division and in the middle of 1990 the market was tantalised by the expectation of similar proposals for the food division although these were subsequently overtaken by the events of August onwards.

Bankers worry

The interim balance sheet for June 1990 showed net debt of £863m and gearing of 93 per cent, little changed from the full year December 1989 position of £800m of net debt and 95 per cent gearing. Net debt was expected to fall in the near future from a number of corporate disposals resulting from the ongoing restructuring of Polly Peck following the major acquisitions of Del Monte and Sansui in 1989.

It is not totally clear whether the collapse in the share price following the aborted buyout caused the fall in confidence among Polly Peck's bankers or whether events proceeded in parallel. However September saw debts being called and uncommitted bank lines withdrawn, causing a major cash flow problem. On 5 October 1990 Polly Peck made a presentation to its bankers and a steering committee of ten banks was formed to represent the more than 100 lenders to Polly Peck. The committee commissioned a report into the company's financial affairs. However as details emerged of the position in Northern Cyprus the banks' standstill agreement collapsed and the company was placed in administration.

Subsequent revelations showed that of £405m cash balances at the interim stage £300m was deposited with banks in Northern Cyprus and Turkey and apparently unavailable for remittance back to the UK. It also became clear that leisure expenditure in Northern Cyprus was considerably higher than expected, with some £230m apparently committed to a number of unspecified new ventures.

It was ironic but perhaps inevitable that Cyprus and Turkey should result in Polly Peck's downfall. After all the group spent much of the 1980s under suspicion over both the quality and quantity of profits arising from the region. However in 1989, the completion of two major acquisitions, Del Monte and Sanui, offered the prospect of totally transforming the group through extending regional strengths to the international markets.

The fall

August 1990 was the month when Polly Peck began to unravel. Press reports pointed to an Inland Revenue investigation into European-based dealing in Polly Peck shares. This began to destabilise the share price which had started the month at 418p, although this situation was rapidly reversed when Asil Nadir announced that he was considering taking Polly Peck private.

However within a week these intentions were withdrawn following representations from unspecified significant shareholders; the Polly Peck share price began to fall, a fall that was accelerated by an adverse Stock Exchange report into the conduct of Mr Nadir and various other directors of the company during the course of the 'buyout', together with press revelations about well-informed European trading in Polly Peck shares.

It was not until the shares has been suspended that the full details of Polly Peck's problems started to emerge. Firstly it became clear that the share price fall was accelerate by banks selling Polly Peck stock held by them as security for loans to Asil Nadir, notwithstanding further buying by Mr Nadir as the share price fell. Secondly, a full-scale financial crisis developed.

Conclusions

With the benefit of hindsight the market appears to have been misled on two counts: firstly the shares appear to have been manipulated and secondly considerable unexpected capital expenditure appears to have taken place in the leisure division.

It is possible that the blocked Cyprus/Turkey balances also fall into this category although examination of the 1988 and 1989 accounts reveals a number of areas of concern. Interest charges were remarkably low in relation to levels of debt; the cash flow particularly in 1988 showed considerable currency impact and finally the tax charge was well below average. In 1989, however, the currency impact was minimal although cash flow remained negative with funds from operations being more than offset by a sharp rise in working capital.

Even now it is difficult to judge whether Polly Peck failed because of malpractice or from fundamental flaws in currency mismatching, working capital controls or even just the absolute level of debt. Had Polly Peck been able to complete its planned 1990 restructuring it is possible that debt pressures could have fallen sharply. However it is clear that capital commitments in the leisure division were rising sharply which would have once more increased the Cyprus exposure and left the group uncomfortably exposed to the then forthcoming recession.

INDEX